Two Wheels To Panamá

WILLIAM CARROLL

Two Wheels To Panamá

by

William Carroll

First Edition

ISBN 0-910390-40-1

Library of Congress Catalog Number 95-94006

Auto Book Press
P.O. Bin 711
San Marcos, California 92079-0711

Printed in the United States of America.

For the many fine people of Mexico

and Central America who knew me not

but helped in so many gracious ways.

TABLE OF CONTENTS

The Cover

This road-building crew in Guatemala was breaking nearby rocks into small pieces to hard-surface a steep section of the Interamerican Highway. The men said they worked two weeks out of each year upgrading nearby roads because they did not have enough money to pay their annual head tax.

ABOUT THIS BOOK

If there was any reason for this ride it should be summed in one word: "Frustration."

By mid-1950 my personal life had become a shambles and the successful business founded a few years before had collapsed. I knew so little about management there was no way to keep expanding and pay bills after the cash flow simmered to a reasonable level. So the business was closed to benefit my creditors.

After satisfying those to whom I owed money there remained a small house. I promptly mortgaged it to a friendly bank by not telling them I planned to buy another motorcycle. But neither the personal or business disaster adequately explains, nor do I remember, how or why the decision was made to tour Latin America for which I had evidenced no previous interest. Nevertheless, the basic plan became to escape the world for a while by riding to Panama, find transportation on a freighter to visit Puerto Rico, then freighter to Florida and bike back to to California. That the program expired in Panama is easily explained. There was no sea shipping between Panama and Puerto Rico and air freight was far beyond the budget.

With bank money in hand I met with two friends, Herb and Lou Caspary, who owned a bike shop in Culver City, California. After adequate soul-searching and discussion we agreed that a big (500 cc) single would be ideal for such a venture because the large engine would make it possible to cruise at acceptable highway speeds. And being a single its vibration frequencies would be so low that body parts would not become numb as was commonly caused by twins of the period. In addition, the thumper's firm power strokes insured low-speed movement over rough terrain. A Triumph Speed Twin was traded off and a B33 ordered with the optional new plunger rear suspension for maximum comfort over the expected rough territory.

While waiting for delivery I met with, and wrote to, a number of magazines to suggest articles to help pay for the trip. The resulting assignments included reports on motorcycling abroad, Central American railroads and U.S. government farm program tests in Costa Rica.

After the bike arrived at Caspary's, Herb supervised my uncrating the beast, completing its assembly and taking the first ride. He rechecked my efforts and suggested break-in techniques which put 700 miles on the clock.

The modifications before departure included bolting three water-proof war-surplus ammo cans around the rear fender assembly to create a platform. They were painted white for coolness and contained film and a camera during the trip. A thick rubber sheet laid over the three was padding for a white steel case which was held in place by web straps. This case was one of the more valuable assets because it could be easily carried into my hotel rooms where, with a large padlock in the hasp, it resisted several attempts to purloin the expensive cameras. It was also comfortable to ship as an obviously very secure metal container.

Another bike modification was the permanent attachment of a two-gallon tube of gasoline to the left of the saddle. It remained in place to Tapachula where the straps broke while traveling on rough dirt. I tossed the tank off into the jungle. On the right side of the BSA frame a canvas tube was fitted to carry the motion picture tripod and tilt head in a vertical position.

A sleeping bag began the journey lashed to the handlebars and ended up being more often tied atop the rear cargo. Somewhere I picked up a pair of leather saddlebags which arrived in Panama stuffed with souvenirs and documents collected for magazine articles to be written.

Spare parts were few on the basis the it would be impossible to carry everything and air shipments could be arranged by telephone or telegram to Culver City. To the BSA tool kit of wrenches and a tire pump I added two spark plugs, magneto breaker points, chain links, a chain breaker and a can of inner tube patches.

By making a running guess at the variety of weather that might be encountered I settled for riding in a war-surplus lightweight aviator's suit which had a wonderful collection of zipper pockets all over the front and arms. Plus wearing a fur-lined leather rider's jacket, red baseball cap and sunglasses. A pair of well-used logger's boots, which had high heels ideal for peg-riding, were given a fresh coating of hot tallow to waterproof the seams. Available in the steel case were two pair of longjohns, a blue suit, white shirts, dress shoes and a tie. The latter items were for expected social occasions which did in fact occur with pleasant frequency.

Photographic equipment was rather extensive. There was a 16 mm Bell & Howell Filmo 70-D bearing a three-lens turret fitted with wide-angle, normal and telephoto lenses. Considerable film was exposed and to date remains in storage. A Kodak Recomar 9 by 12 cm sheet film camera was carried to handle the exposure of Kodachrome sheet film. Some of these color shots been published and two are in this book as the Guatemala City cathedral and wood-cutting boatman in San Salvador.

The most often-used camera was a Rolleiflex 2-1/4 by 2-1/4 which exposed 120 size black and white Agfa Supreme roll film. Over a thousand negatives proved useful from which a selection of prints was made for this book.

ABOUT THIS BOOK

The Recomar rode in one of the white containers on the back of the bike. The motion picture camera in a soft bag, and the Rolleiflex in its hard case, dangled around my neck from beginning to end. After the mailing experience in Mexico City all films were air-shipped from the airport postoffice of each national capital, to the U.S. for processing and temporary storage.

It's hard to believe now but maps for guidance were on a catch-as-catch-can basis. An Auto Club giveaway led me from Los Angles to El Paso. The first overnight was with friends in Holtville, California. On the next day the route passed along land which was 220 feet below sea level and near what remained of a wood plank road across desert sand between Yuma and San Diego. In El Paso a day was used to give the bike a thorough inspection and enjoy a superb American-style steak dinner served in the kitchen of a Chinese restaurant. When I first purchased gasoline in Mexico I picked up a Pemex highway map of the nation. Later, as I entered each country in turn, I would first look for an Esso station as they had the only quickly available free highway maps. Gasoline and oil were never really a problem except when a town (such as in Nicaragua) had no gasoline at all.

After I entered Mexico without being able to speak Spanish it became a matter of learn or perish. I learned fast and in Mexico City could find a place to sleep and eat with little trouble. By Guatemala it was possible to conduct a simple conversation and the language situation became better the farther I traveled.

Two Wheels To Panamá is a condensed version of a massive book manuscript which was completed a few months after my arrival in Panama. In addition the daily journal, comprising ten spiral-bound notebooks, contributed interesting odds and ends which had not found their way into the manuscript. All the still camera films were reviewed as another source of information. A few names have been changed to protect the innocent and not so innocent.

When crossing a border resulted in a rubber stamp blessing my passport, the official approval has been inserted at the beginning or end of each section. Scattered throughout this report are bracketed mileages such as (4320 miles). These reflect total trip mileage to that point and do not indicate Interamerican Highway miles or distances between specific points. Currency conversions are approximate at the rate of exchange in existence in 1950-51 and in no way reflect the exchange rates of today's market.

The cost of a gallon of gasoline or quart of oil was about 50 cents. The BSA turned in a neat average of 62 miles to the gallon. In Panama there remained about 1/8th-inch of tread on the front tire and 3/32nd-inch on the rear. There were 32 days of riding from one major overnight to the next. Total cost of food, hotels and gasoline for the 32 days of point-to-point travel was $178.38, plus 75 cents for repairing the flat tire in El Salvador. These figures are separate from expenses of the many long stays in the interesting capital cities. This balance of time on the journey was enjoyed as a city tourist or for side trips to points of interest.

At that time I weighed in at 175 pounds. The cargo totaled 125 pounds. This was barely acceptable on the basis that the B33 fender was designed for a pillion seat and slender second rider. The marginal overload became evident when I discovered that by quickly twisting the handlebars I could cause the rear of the bike to crack-the-whip. Perhaps it was this flexibility that kept everything together when the going became unreasonably rough. In later production years BSA increased the frame tube's thickness.

Though it has no direct connection, two years after arriving in Panama I drove back to the States from Nicaragua in a Singer roadster. Along the bike's route there were many who remembered my passing earlier on the BSA and made me welcome again. In 1967-68 I drove from Alaska to Rio de Janerio which included the Interamerican Highway through Mexico and Central America. Except for Talisman it had all changed. At that time a drive from Los Angeles to Panama could be accomplished in a little over two weeks on pavement almost all the way.

In conclusion it is worth pointing out that throughout the bike trip there were many local people who stepped forward to help. Such as the businessman who led me to a hotel, Charley and his uniques, the priests of Guatemala and El Salvador, the truck driver who carried my luggage into Tegucigalpa, the trucker who filled my gas tank in Nicaragua and the *sabaneros* who towed me out of too-deep Costa Rican rivers. Without them all, and the many others, *Two Wheels To Panamá* could not have been successful or the story written.

Would I do it again?

No!

But there's a different ride I'd like to take if I thought the bod would hold together.

Bill Carroll

It was December 14, and 970 miles from Los Angeles, when I paid a dime to ride over the El Paso, Texas, toll bridge into Mexico's Ciudad Juarez border control station. With the assistance of not speaking or reading Spanish I promptly proceeded to bring up the rear of a line that was for permits to leave the country. Twenty minutes later an English-speaking officer effected a rescue and provided a card that said, in effect, "I am a tourist...if lost give help." A cursory inspection of baggage and motorcycle insurance was adequate for him to point me 1700 miles further south to Mexico City.

Once outside Juarez city limits the bike was flying low past frequent kilometer road markers, indicating decreasing distance from Mexico City, when a blind curve swept us past a cluster of buildings. The concurrent sound of shots was quickly augmented by the squeal of braking motorcycle tires. With both feet on the ground I very cautiously looked back over my shoulder to find a group of Mexican officers, with guns in their hands, laughing at me. They had not been shooting at the BSA but were target practicing at pebbles placed on the highway. I made a very careful U-turn to give the officers an opportunity to inspect everything I carried and allow my riding further into their country. While repacking my cargo a pair of elderly ladies stopped, presented papers and were also approved to proceed. One woman had troubles. She asked an officer where the "rest room" could be found. Not understanding enough English the pistol-practicing gentleman smiled brightly in recognition that the lady had asked a question. "Si senora, to Mexico City...that way," he replied with a grand gesture toward the highway leading south to the capital city.

The first lunch stop, in a rural village for which I have no name, included understanding that without a knowledge of Spanish I would often be in trouble ordering a reasonable meal.

Great distances in northern Mexico
were through barren areas where the infrequent
village was a collection of crude adobe structures.

Two-hundred miles further south on Mexico's Route 45 I cruised into Chihuahau and was dismayed to discover that a doctors' convention had filled the major hotels. Fortunately a friendly service station attendant provided directions to a small hotel where a room was available for less than a dollar. But there was nothing nearby that slightly resembled a place to eat and my questions to the hotel clerk were answered with floods of unusable Spanish. Finally he escorted me down a nearby alley to the Cafe Rits, pushed me through the doorway, shouted a Spanish command to an invisible person and left. A tiny woman of indeterminate age appeared from the back, decided that I was hungry and displayed the menu. Still no dice. I couldn't read a word. Taking the bull by the horns I explored her kitchen and opened boxes, cupboards and refrigerator, to locate eggs, chicken, steaks, canned goods and vegetables. A lot of pointing and it was settled. Soon salad, steak and fried potatoes, plus something the color of coffee, appeared on the table. I ate, enjoyed an excellent beer, paid 40¢ (U.S.) and picked my way back through the alley to the hotel.

The following day was uneventful except for being picked up by an English-speaking policeman who insisted I meet the chief of police and inspect their new headquarters. This took three hours. Tearing myself loose from such unwelcome official attention and riding another 200 miles at full bore carried me into the town of Parral (1420 miles). While I was searching for hotels a boy on a bicycle peddled up alongside and, in English, inquired of my needs. The young man was the town's unofficial guide and had been sitting on a nearby hill to watch the main road through a pair of old opera glasses. On seeing this *turista* head into town he had coasted down hill on his bike to catch me. A good hotel was found, the BSA parked in the back yard and my bod showered. Henry, at 75¢ (U.S.) and a free dinner, was a most entertaining companion who offered an introduction to the mayor, an interview with the newspaper (because my business card identified me as a journalist) and a visit to the local whore house. I settled for the interview. After expounding on visiting Mexico, to Parral's only reporter, I visited three radio stations before Henry escorted me to promenade night.

A church facing the central square played recorded music through loud speakers hung in the belfry while unmarried young men and girls paraded around the square. The men, arm in arm and two or three abreast, walked counterclockwise. The girls, in twos or more, walked in the opposite direction. Henry and I walked and saw everything Parral had to offer, all of which was chaperoned by watchful mothers gossiping on park benches. Henry explained that anyone could smile and flirt as a specific girl approached and she might smile or wink in response. If you could handle this for several weeks, and the girl of your choice saw no one she liked better, come Sunday a bouquet of flowers might be presented at church. If she accepted the flowers the lucky young man could walk her around the plaza and make with conversation. If pleased, the girl might invite him to her home after church so father and mother could inspect the new prospect. My plans did not include moving to Mexico so I thanked Henry for his guidance and left.

The Tropic of Cancer is 23-1/2 degrees north of the equator and the northernmost latitude reached by the overhead sun, perchance you really wanted to know.

At my next overnight stop in Durango (1693 miles) a Mexican businessman led me to a hotel, Mex. $10 ($1.20 U.S.), by driving ahead in his new Jeep. While following him I saw policemen patrolling the city streets riding two-up on Harley-Davidsons. Later I met an overnight watchman (above) who protected curbside cars for 25 *centavos* each. By myself I learned that potent Mexican rum was Mex. $1 (12¢ U.S.) a shot, *cantinas* had an open urinal in a back corner of the room so beer drinkers wouldn't lose time running back and forth and that my hotel maintained some of its dinner livestock in the interior patio. At least the small flock of noisy turkeys under my room window disappeared, one by one, into the kitchen during the early evening dining hours.

Zacatecas, one of Mexico's most colorful colonial towns, was good for the next overnight and a subsequent four-day stay at Mex. $12 ($1.50 U.S.) a night for room and board. The motorcycle proved handy for visiting out-of-the-way sights such as the mission atop a nearby hill. There seemed to be only one pathway and up I rode. To my chagrin this was a foot path and other visitors showed no enthusiasm for stepping aside as I motored past. At the top I found a perfectly good paved road on the far side of the building. The air was so clear and countryside so quiet I could hear people talk on Zacatecas' streets far below.

One evening Bob Wiseman, a young American college student, and I decided to sample the town's nightlife. We tried several *cantinas* before noticing a small *cantina* sign at the far end of a very dark stair-step alley. We decided to investigate. As we left the illuminated street a series of bird whistles arose from around our feet. Our eyes became accustomed to the dimness and we saw people curled up on every step. They all must have been wide awake for as we progressed down the alley their warning whistling preceded and followed us.

This wide-ranging view of Zacatecas is from the foot-path leading up to the Mission that overlooks the community.

An hour later we left the *cantina* when the bartender offered free drinks and the other patrons were obviously waiting for our misfortune to happen. The same whistling escorted us up the stair-step alley to the main street. A dance hall received our staggering frames, then another *cantina* and at 4 a.m. we were arguing with two nightwatchmen in the central square. They tried to convince us to buy their next meal because we were having such a wonderful time in their town. I thanked them for their interest and settled for finding my hotel with its *cama matrimonial*, as a double bed was called.

While wandering around town the next day I was intrigued by a traffic jam of stopped Mexican busses with their drivers neither blowing horns or arguing. The cause of this unique situation arrived slowly from around a nearby corner. Leading a procession of simple dignity was a bareheaded funeral director wearing khaki trousers and a leather jacket. He carried a wooden cross from which dangled a slip of paper with the deceased person's name and age written on it. Following were four barefoot pallbearers in worn blue denim trousers and jackets who carried a simple carpenter-built coffin covered with thin black cloth. It was followed by a middle-age man, hat in hand, shedding unrestrained tears with every step of his bare feet. Behind him four boys, ranging from about 16 to 24, quietly followed their father in a two-mile walk to the nearest burial ground. The bus drivers and I waited until the procession was a block away before taking up the usually hurried business of living.

The next highway section was from Zacatecas to Queretaro over a mountain range where both pair of long underwear did yeoman's duty keeping the frame warm. So much time was spent poking along and taking more scenic pictures that I arrived in town after dark. Few of the streets were illuminated and while cautiously bumping over cobblestones I was startled to face a red light, without visible means of support, waving in the air some 15 feet above the street. As we came together the light proved to be over a horse-drawn wagon in which the driver was holding a red lantern high above his head to warn other traffic of his existence.

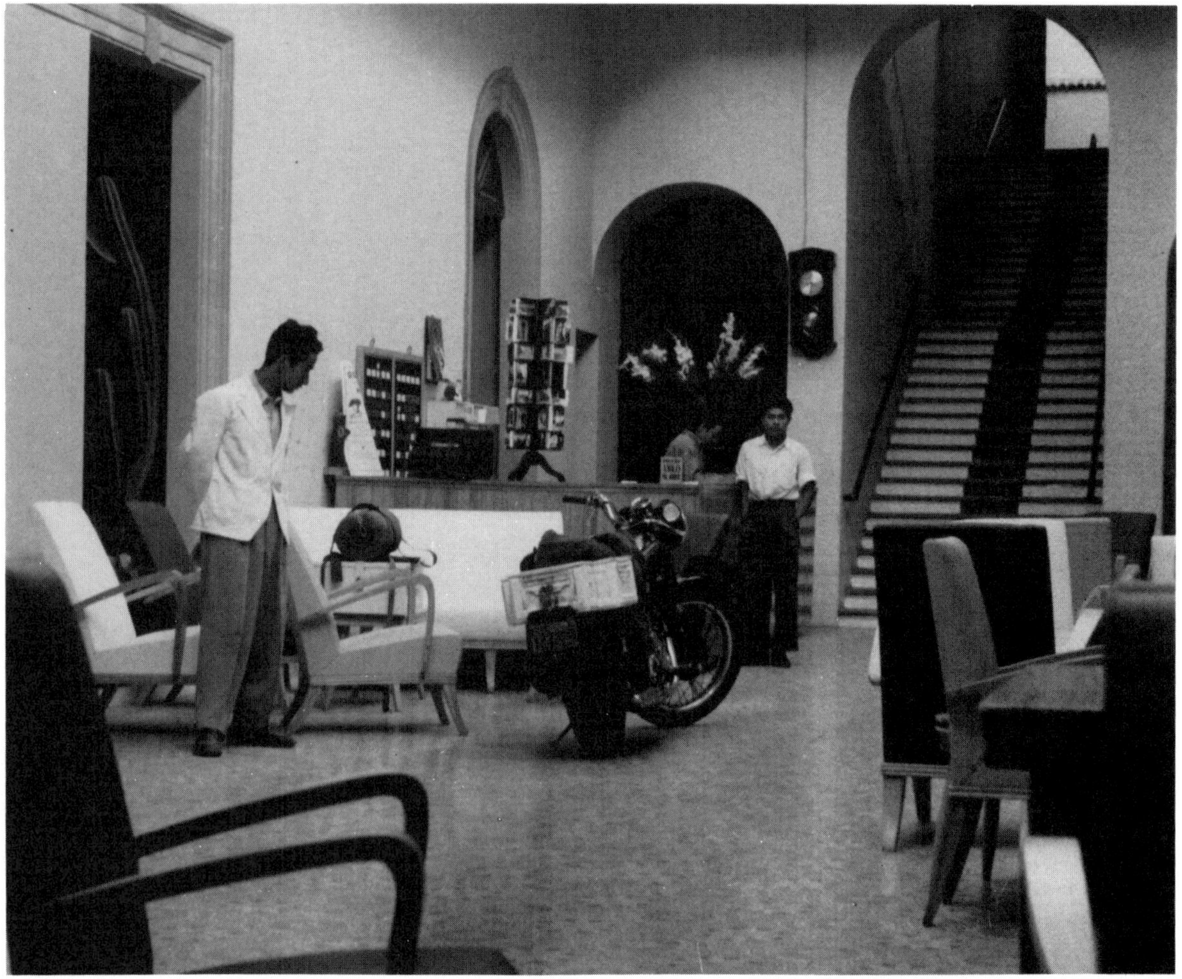

The dubious dining room help had to decide on the best way to move the bike into the hotel's liquor storage cellar.

At the first hotel in Queretaro (2203 miles) I arranged for a room before being told that all garages were closed so there was no place for the bike. My lack of enthusiasm for overnight curb-side parking was understandable and the clerk arranged for a pair of waiters to put the BSA into the hotel liquor cellar. The following morning I decided to present a letter of introduction to the local chief of police. While I was waiting in his office at the *Palacio Municipal* the hotel clerk showed up with four copies of the guest list. One copy was for the local police file, one for the Federal police, one for Mexico's tourist bureau and the last copy was initialed and returned for retention by the hotel as a record of the evening's guests.

After lunch, while taking motion pictures, I noticed that park benches displayed metal tags listing their donor and that sound vibrations from tolling church bells sent tiny waves across water in the plaza fountain. More interesting were two very attractive young ladies on the shady side of a nearby street selling Red Cross badges to support a local charity. To better photograph their efforts I tried to explain that the sunny side of the street would be a great benefit for color film. In five minutes my poor Spanish convinced them of nothing and they succeeded in selling me a badge for an American dollar. Business over, the taller of the two asked the other, in perfect American-eze, "Do you imagine that he speaks English?"

I stammered, "Just a little."

Following that intelligent response the smaller girl told her friend, "He is probably a Frenchman." With that they hurried away.

A bull fight that afternoon was highlighted by the bull jumping over the arena barrier and chasing a soldier stationed between the barrier and safety fence. Said soldier was so panic-stricken he fled halfway around the circle before shouts of his fellows convinced him to jump back over the barrier into the arena where the bull was not. The audience applauded his performance as much as subsequent bullfights.

Rural villages without electricity were visited by this converted bus which showed motion pictures against the largest white building.

Later a Mexican matador told me that he had been educated in Kansas and performed in the bull ring on a contract that included hospitalization, retirement coverage and life insurance. For risking his neck he claimed a monthly income of about $1000 (U.S.) from which he supported himself and maintained a protege learning the art of bull fighting.

While I was munching on a leathery pastry menued as *Hot Cakes* the next morning there was a small commotion at the adjacent table where an American couple was ordering breakfast in English. As they were having no luck I used my miniscule Spanish to help. They were grateful when the waiter brought them the right toast and eggs, which just happened to be the same breakfast the waiter and I had organized with difficulty the day before. During the ensuing conversation the visitors told me about touring Mexico for two months but not yet being able to order a complete meal. As I left the dining room a countryman came into the lobby with about 20 live chickens slung over his shoulder. Our hotel manager stopped his bookkeeping chores to feel every chicken, bargain like a fishwife for lower prices and buy eight of the best for dinner that evening.

An invitation had been extended by the town's social leader, who also owned the hotel, to attend her private posada party, which traditionally took place during the Christmas holiday period. I was told she owned more than one hotel, several business buildings and had a large family. That evening I wandered around Queretaro, watched a parade, listened to church choirs and finally arrived at the address given me. The dark, narrow doorway fronted a twisty flight of dirty one-person wide stairs behind an open steel gate. The second flight of stairs was a revelation. Wide tile treads led up to a lovely plant-lined patio that was noisy with people. Introductions followed and for some reason or other I was soon holding a drink while standing near a green dress filled with a most remarkable body. Both were managed by Suzanna, one of the hostess' four daughters "...and would you like to tour the house?" There were living rooms, bed rooms, patios, the huge kitchen with a charcoal stove and three cooks, a dining room with a buffet spread and a wonderful overlook of the town's central plaza from a front balcony. Unfortunately it was impossible to remain there long because one of the bullfighters had a local charmer backed into the darkest corner.

A group of street musicians came into the living room and while furniture was being moved against the walls Suzanna suggested we check her mother's liquor supply. Sampling disclosed that labels were on the proper bottles and the contents would be safe for the other guests. Music was on the breeze by the time we returned to the living room and began to dance. About 30 minutes of this and the orchestra stopped for a short intermission. When they began anew with traditional Mexican melodies two guests moved onto the floor, a professional dancer from Mexico City and her local boy friend. Another woman began to dance with her husband and the four put on a stirring exhibition of folk dancing. As the exhibition concluded one of Suzanna's brothers came to her and said something about *El Bufalo*.

The evening holiday parade featured a number of well-done floats. This one carried a choir through city streets while they sang carols.

In one second flat I was alone and trying to figure out why until the reason passed through the door and headed in my direction. It was about 6’4" and 240 pounds of muscle led by my moments-ago companion. Introductions were next and I made the acquaintance of Suzanna’s fiance, known as "The Buffalo" because of his strength and size. After they moved on to visit with other guests I counted the fingers of my right hand. There were five though they felt as one.

The next morning I left for Mexico City as soon as my headache was in traveling condition. On the way I parked by the roadside to write notes of the previous day and in a few minutes noticed that the bike and I were being circled by a flock of large buzzards. Apparently when it doesn’t move they consider it a possible dinner so I rode away before hunger overcame their wisdom. It was a cool journey while passing through mountains near the 6500-foot mark before the highway brought me down into the Mexico City basin on December 28.

After checking into a hotel I intended the subsequent dinner to be something of a celebration of arrival. In a nearby cafe I ordered beer, filet mignon and ice cream. The steak arrived with a mound of fries and a small pile of chopped green beans. As there were only a few greens I decided to eat them before tackling the steak. It was my major error of the day. They were not green beans but chopped green chili peppers. My mouth was illuminated by the glow of fire consuming human flesh and two glasses of water in rapid succession failed to keep my eyes from spraying tears everywhere. The waiter was so worried he pounded my back with mischievous concerned enthusiasm. It helped.

One chore in Mexico City was to mail exposed films to the States for processing. The package was prepared, sealed and addressed before I went to the central post office. Of 20 different windows I selected the one with a short line leading to an Airmail sign. The window clerk was apologetic in explaining that her scale was much too small to weigh my package and that I would have to go to the adjacent window. This meant more standing in the other line to have the package weighed. But no stamps. They were only available from another clerk who sold me $22.40 (U.S.) worth. But I was still not able to mail the stuff. "Go to Window 55 down the hall." the clerk instructed. Window 55 looked at the address, said "No" and wrote down 43. At Window 43 the lady clerk obtained my name and address with the help of several willing interpreters and placed a *Registrada* sticker near the stamps. Then back to Window 55 who said, "No, go to 58." This was the *Aduanera* (Customs inspector) who had to look inside. I opened the parcel and displayed the contents before being loaned a pot of glue to seal the whole works again for mailing. But he could not take letters and directed me to the center of the building. This I found by myself, dropped airmail letters in a slot marked *Exterior* and left the building a free man 55 minutes after entering to buy a few stamps. When I returned to the hotel it appeared my belongings had been shifted about but nothing was missing except my tourist card which I decided was no longer needed as I was now in the nation’s capital city.

The best I can say about those who knocked the BSA over is that they reparked it off to one side near the boundary fence.

Another education was telephoning the BSA dealer in Mexico City, the oldest British trader in Mexico, who marketed several makes of motorcycles. After three tries the number was answered with *Bueno* (Good) which was the polite manner of reporting that we had achieved a usable connection. I explained my desire to visit them and was given directions. Ten minutes later in the hotel parking lot I found the bike had been knocked over by a careless driver and I was madder than hell. The left peg rubber was torn and the tank and chain case bruised.

The importer's shop made repairs while I obtained article material about motorcycles in Mexico. A new Triumph twin sold for $630 (U.S.) and most of the approximately 5000 machines in Mexico had been sold for cash. Racing and organized cycle sports did not exist and police motor officers gutted Harley mufflers to make more noise. On the way back to the hotel a brand new road hazard was experienced: missing manhole covers. This scared hell out of me as they were the last thing one expects to be dangerously absent from city streets.

The number of beggars was astounding and it was soon learned that the only way to not be approached was to never permit one to catch your eye. However in the Central Park a small boy was so persistent I offered to match him for 25 *centavos* (4¢ U.S.). The kid laughed at the prospect of a tourist gambling with him, reached into his ragged clothes, dredged up a coin and we tossed. I lost, paid off and was propositioned to try again; double or nothing. When his kind offer was declined the kid rubbed his elbow to tell me I was a cheapskate and ran off.

Beggars were everywhere in Mexico City, which added little to the pleasure of visiting the many historic sites and splendid museums.

This is the Tree of the Sad Night (El Arbol de la Noche Triste) under which Cortes sat and wept (1519) after the Spaniard's disastrous retreat from Tenochtitlan.

The floating gardens of Xochimilco are known to date from before arrival of the Spanish in 1519. Today their restaurants and barge trips are a tourist attraction.

The low mountain range in the distance was known locally as "The Sleeping Lady" because of its buxom appearance.

One night later in a restaurant which had call buttons on the table to summon a waiter, the sound of grind-organ music floated in from the street. This carried on for a minute or so then stopped before a boy of 10 or 12 came through the restaurant carrying a crank handle and begging. He hit everyone in the place then left, to be replaced by a girl of eight or nine carrying the same crank handle. She was followed by a slightly younger girl and finally a child of four or five came through. Her technique was terrific. She toddled up to the table, held onto the edge with grubby hands and watched every bite of food leave the plate and enter your mouth. She was highly successful adding coins to her dirty cigar box until the manager ran her out. When I went outside I found the performance being repeated at a bar further down the street. It was a well-organized operation. Father turned the organ, had a spare crank handle for the kids to carry and mother dispatched them in sequence to maintain a profitable schedule.

I was 3080 miles from home the morning I left Mexico City for Puebla on my first section of *La Carretera Interamericana* (The Interamerican Highway) which enters Mexico from Laredo, Texas. (I had ridden in from El Paso.) From Puebla to Atlixo was through lovely mountains heavily populated by unfenced livestock, which had left numerous slippery calling cards on the highway. Atlixo's best hotel (3185 miles) used padlocks to protect the doors, floors were of concrete tiles and the water pitcher and wash bowl showed damage a hundred years old. This time the BSA was

The huge Atlixo hotel room had a mind-boggling collection of antiquities including hand-crafted floor tiles, iron wash-bowl stand and wall-mounted light switch.

In the Oaxaca public market there were stalls vending every conceivable necessity including tiny boxes of detergent barely adequate for one washing.

parked in a hallway between the hotel barbershop and bar. This proved to be an opportunity for guests to test the seat, push every button in sight and discuss the California license plate. Here I was introduced to the community toilet where hotel guests, owner and servants mingled in noisy fraternity without regard for gender.

The following day was a pleasant journey through land that appeared rich and well farmed. Low mountains were covered with scrub pine and each tiny village featured a white-washed church as the largest building. My overnight was in Oaxaca (3440 miles), which was noted for its woven rugs. Street vendors all assured me they did their own weaving, though one man said he was selling for his sister. I was more impressed by the variety of huge knives and machetes for sale in the public market. Most of the blades were engraved with designs and motto's of exceptional beauty.

If you could not write, for a small fee the public letter-writer would type your message. This Avisos board on a market-place wall carried religious notices and obituaries.

THROUGH MEXICO

Writing on the bridge reports that Enrique Vargas is the father of F.F. Higareo. There were many of these interesting religious structures along the highways of Mexico.

South of Mexico City the Interamerican Highway took me through areas of barren land which displayed stark beauty highlighted by infrequent villages and churches.

The next day involved more miles of beautiful mountain scenery punctuated by less-frequent villages nestled in canyons or hanging from hillsides, each with the inevitable church. Villages near the highway often had a gas station featuring a rack of 55-gallon drums from which a hand pump would fill tanks for 47¢ (U.S.) a gallon. At one of them I learned that rural gasoline was colored red and kerosene green to keep locals from blowing themselves up by pouring the wrong fuel into their lanterns.

After leaving the mountainous area the road dropped down across a valley to a cattle-disease disinfecting station. The motorcycle was washed with DDT spray, my shoes were inspected and two soldiers insisted on having their picture taken. Once the shutter clicked they were happy and demonstrated no interest in prints or payment. Another mile and I entered Tehuantepec. The town's major roadside restaurant and hotel was from a Florida nightmare in which rows of bright pink plaster cabins were surrounded by flower beds cluttered with nothing but unfriendly weeds. The luncheon was good tourist-style food with entertainment by a lady and her husband at the next table. They had been in Mexico for six weeks and after ordering the complete luncheon relaxed to await their meal. The soup arrived but the lady did not like lentils so the bowl was returned. Then salad but someone told her not to eat salads in Mexico so she ate none. Next was the delicious main course of roast beef, potatoes, beans, rice, rolls

He not only did a great job of washing BSA machinery but also reduced braking efficiency to an absolute zero, as was discovered later.

Although it may be informal, this sign serves its purpose well for drivers who do not read and for bike riders who are not overly cautious.

and butter. She knew all about hoof and mouth disease, potato bugs, non-enriched bread, non-pasturized butter and did not care for rice or beans. Her plate was returned to the kitchen uneaten and a pudding was served for desert. Much to the lady's sorrow it was chocolate and that was constipating. Her husband enjoyed the same meal, was still alive and appeared little worried about his wife's problems. They decided that a bottle of sparking water might be good for her. However, due to a mis-translation from English to Spanish the waitress brought and opened a cola drink, which the lady could not drink because of the sugar content. After the couple left we remaining guests exchanged comments on how important it would be for them to hurry back to the States before she starved to death in the midst of plenty.

Until now Mexico's highways had been excellent pavement but just a few miles past lunch a road construction project upset the reputation. At that time when a road was built the crews leveled the right-of-way, laid a six-inch layer of fist-sized broken rock, then ignored it for a few months so that passing vehicles would compact the surface. It was rough riding until I noticed that the shoulder was wide enough for two-wheel traveling.

After 12 miles of construction the route became tired old pavement with a few streams to ford. As it was late afternoon I began to flat out wherever possible but darkness fell when I was nowhere in particular so I turned on the headlight. Not a glimmer. The rough construction had broken both filaments. The stars were bright and the next 18 miles were ridden on

Riding up this road in the dark was no fun. Nor waking to find a deep ravine just a few feet beyond the sleeping bag.

pavement barely visible between bordering trees. This bit of madness led me upward to a low mountain pass where, near the summit, the asphalt gave way to a narrow sandy twisting roadway. A fading flashlight held in one hand was little help as it was too often pointing in the wrong direction. This section was so bad that I was constantly plagued by piles of dirt or serious depressions not visible in the darkness.

Enough was enough and after about a half hour of misery I gave up at a sharp turn in an area of flat grassland untouched by the road crew. The bike was parked between the roadway and my sleeping bag and I crawled in. Within a few minutes a herd of sheep was driven by, followed by of a wheezy truck I heard long before it lumbered around the corner. Finally my sagging body gave up and the next sound was from a horseman singing as he rode past in the morning sun. I untangled from the sleeping bag, rolled over on my back and sat up to be greeted by a terrifying spectacle.

In all innocence I had parked by the very edge of a sheer cliff and two roll-overs could have dumped me into a ravine about 200 feet deep. Under other circumstances my speed of departure would have been funny but I was not about to trust luck any further. There might be a landslide or suchlike and I wanted nothing more than to be far gone. After I crested the summit, the dirt roadway proved to be a first-gear downhill hassle to the outskirts of Arriaga. Turns were so sharp and occurred so often that two truck drivers grinding their way uphill were actually hugging the proper side of the road...which in rural Mexico was something seldom observed by man or beast.

In portions of southern Mexico women
were often found doing laundry in the town's nearest
river and drying clothes on random bushes and rocks.

When I was advised to follow
cobblestone paving into the countryside,
this is what local guidance was all about.

Arriaga (3765 miles) was said to be the end of the line as far as motored transportation was concerned. Almost everyone told me that *La Carretera Interamericana* had not been completed further south and the railroad was the only way to reach Tapachula near the Guatemalan border. However, one of the many maps picked up along the way showed a route between Arriaga and Tapachula that the Guatemalan consul said he "thought" was usable. I decided the map was an updated version of the area but strangely enough no one in Arriaga knew of such a roadway.

The police department's desk officer insisted that I must take the train and pointed out the railroad station from where I shipped most of my baggage to Tapachula. Then trying to be a little smarter (read as "dumber") instead of asking how to reach Tapachula I inquired about a road to the next town. This was easy. All I had to do was follow a cobblestone street, ford a river underneath the railroad bridge and dust along nice smooth dirt, thinking how easy this was going to be. But not for long. The dirt became progressively worse. I parked while a herd of cattle was driven past then waited for two squealing ox carts following the cattle. In 16 miles I forded seven small streams and gave way for two more herds of cattle before I chugged into Tonalia, a very small village with the nicest cold beer I've ever needed.

Local bar flies pointed me toward another cobblestone street in the general direction of Tapachula with the next small village said to be about 25 miles further on. Now the going really became rough. Wheel ruts petered out in a mile or two and the route was either a footpath or random cart tracks between adjacent ranches. There were more streams to ford and meadow gates to open and close while I blessed the heat. After splashing through a nice wide river without trouble I parked the bike under a shade tree with a family of pigs who didn't object when I flopped on their grass to rest.

A few minutes farther there was another stream of good size which seemed about the same depth as the earlier one. All went well until near the far bank the front tire struck a submerged rock, twisted sideways and buried itself into a deep hole. I picked me out of the water and surveyed what could have been serious damage. The rear tire had spun a hole into the sand, the crankcase was resting on its own rock and deep water swirled around the front end. A few healthy grunts lifted the front free of obstructions, then the rear tire was shoved onto a rocky base for better traction. One kick brought the engine to life and we bumped out onto dry land. Emptying water from my boots took a few minutes before we continued through what appeared to be uninhabited jungle.

Custom home building includes the selection of posts with a fork at the top into which tie beams can be laid and rafters attached.

The pathway narrowed even more and appeared to have been traveled for years somewhat as a tunnel of vegetation. An hour or so later I stopped for a bottle of soda from my knapsack. A slight noise caught my attention and I found an old man with an axe and his son with a machete standing close behind while observing my actions. I offered cigarettes and tried to start a conversation. Apparently they knew more Indian than Spanish, or my Spanish was so bad they could understand none of it. Other than this chance meeting there was no one on the footpath. After many hours of riding the deep sand had become so tiring that I was having trouble. Once it was much too much to even hold the bike up and we both tumbled onto the path where I sprawled like a sack of flour.

Doubts began to suggest returning to Arriaga. Here I was, six hours out, nearly 40 miles into a jungle, not really sure where I was, and no sign of habitation. A half-hour more riding and the doubts were shifting to worry when a thatched hut hove into view. It was peopled by ten children and one woman, who could not understand anything I said. In desperation I used every word, English and Spanish, that came to mind to describe a railroad that was supposed to be in the area. Suddenly she turned on and began to *Si* me to death while pointing up another sandy path. She used the Spanish word for railway (*ferrocarril*) to convince me that it was only a short distance farther through more of the endless nowhere.

It's an understatement to say that I was surprised to find these two standing behind me in this tropic land of few habitations and even fewer signs of civilization.

As the train pulled out of Tres Picos it was easy to accept the railroad as the better means of reaching the Mexican frontier with Guatemala.

This was great news. I plowed through more sand, around a bend in the narrow pathway and was suddenly riding along the short dusty main street of Tres Picos. At the far end there was a gorgeous pair of rusty old rails and the railroad station. I bought a bottle of warm pop and was given the bad news. No road or walking path existed to the village 40 miles further on. There were no hotels in Tres Picos and nine buildings I could see from the station were it.

I was advised to take the train if I was serious about going to Tapachula. Refreshed by the drink I decided to ride between the rails to the next village. This was a good idea near the station where spaces between the ties were filled with dirt, but the further from town I bumped the less dirt and the further apart the ties. About a half-mile of this foolishness changed my mind in favor of saving tires and we bumped back to town and arms of the local policeman. I explained very carefully that I was only waiting for the train, when did it arrive and did he smoke cigarettes? American coffin nails were worth their weight in gold and in this instance a package of 20 could only be considered a gesture of friendship and not a bribe.

He directed me back to the station where the agent patiently explained charges of Mex. $25 ($3 U.S.) for the cycle and Mex. $20 ($2.50 U.S.) for me to Tapachula. I did not have enough Mexican money so the bike was shipped COD and I bought a one-way ticket. The train was long overdue but still would not arrive for another hour, which provided time to check both cantinas for food, without luck.

However news of my arrival must have spread through the village because on leaving the last bar a pretty little girl grabbed my arm, said "Come" and led me to a nearby house. The family was already seated ready for lunch and I was invited to join them. My host, a man of about 25, sat at the head of the table wearing a felt hat, which remained in place as he introduced me to everyone. To my right were two hired men and the grandmother. On the other side of the table were three more hired men. Lunch was stewed meat in thick brown gravy with beans, rice and tortillas. My host spit his inedible bones and gristle floorward for an emaciated dog. I left mine on the plate. Other members of the family, including my girl guide, either cooked at the outside fireplace or hung around the doorway to watch us eat. We were waiting for grandmother to complete her toothless chomping when a locomotive whistle blew and it was courteously suggested that I hurry to the station. An offer to pay for the meal was refused in no uncertain terms and the young man said he was proud to be of help. I ran for the rails where a freight train was entering the siding to wait for the overdue passenger train. There was time to grab several packages of cigarettes and return to my host who accepted them for his family and the hired men. After handshaking with everyone within calling distance I was sent back to the railroad station.

Finally an ancient locomotive, with its whistle blowing so continually that I was afraid the train would stop for lack of steam, appeared ahead of two freight cars, a baggage car and several tired coaches. Its arrival at Tres Picos' activated hangers-on to unload beer, cement and a few small boxes of freight. Meanwhile the station agent was busy telling the train's baggage man about my motorcycle and how I had tried to ride the ties. Completion of unloading put a stop to their conversation and someone produced a 12-inch wide plank about ten feet long, which was propped from the ground to the baggage car door. Everyone became quiet as the baggage man told me to ride the plank up into his car. I declined to perform and four villagers helped balance and push the bike upward. Inside the car we were lashing the bike between boxes of beer and sacks of rice when the train started as my luggage was tossed through the door. I rode with the bike until we stopped 45 minutes further on.

It was a fast run back to the last car, labeled *Primera Clase* (First Class) where I climbed aboard and took the only vacant seat. There were bottle caps all over the floor, people were sleeping in seats, a dice game was in progress, a red-haired female tourist in a sheer blouse was pleasing Mexican youths and two salesmen were busily swapping stories. The train started to the tune of irregular rail joints with the brakeman standing on the rear steps while relieving his bladder at the passing jungle. No one worried because the toilet was plugged and leaking outrageous odors over the floor.

I ordered a cool beer from the vendor and watched the circus. We were running full blast at about 15 miles an hour while the coach danced up, down, and sideways, with the front always moving in a different direction than the rear. Such lurches from track irregularities were enough to make bracing yourself in the seat absolutely necessary. This was somewhat uncomfortable until I discovered several empty beer bottles wedged behind the seat cushions. At most village stops children entered the coach, paraded along the aisle then waited by the steps to jump after the train began to move, with the bravest boy jumping last. Larger villages produced food vendors with such goodies as fresh coconuts, sweets, hard-boiled eggs and warm tortillas filled with wonderful food aromas. Language difficulties confined my intake to beer or falling asleep from accumulated exhaustion and the lack of anything else to do.

About 1 A.M. we groaned to a halt in Hutlixia, the largest village so far. A marimba band heading home from a closing cantina stopped to serenade the train for coins and applause. Both were enough to wake the dead and when we banged into a farmer's cow two miles out of town I was alert enough to walk ahead and watch the proceedings. Such accidents were said to be a common occurrence for which the engine crew was prepared. They removed a long timber from the tender, levered the deceased animal off the tracks then restarted with toots of the whistle to honor the vanquished bovine.

A little over two hours later, at 3:45 in the morning, we rattled into the border town of Tapachula a few miles from the Guatemalan border on the *Rio Suchiate*. I followed the salesmen to the Hotel International, was given a room and bug-spray gun for Mex. $25 ($3 U.S.) a day with all meals. After sleep, and breakfast in the dining room, it was only a short walk to the railroad station. On Sunday it was open only for ticket sales and and an extra fee was requested to have a key turned in the freighthouse lock. Mex. $5 (60¢ U.S.) changed hands. Bike and luggage were collected, I checked out of the hotel and rode 12 miles of excellent pavement to Mexico's Talisman exit control station at the frontier with Guatemala (3814 miles).

The central business district of Tapachula was somewhat more impressive than the railroad yard from where the bike was collected.

Talisman, Mexico's brindle-colored border-control station, was a site I was to become unpleasantly familiar with. On arrival the immigration officer would not pass me into Guatemala because I could not produce the tourist card stolen in Mexico City. The passport was in order and motorcycle entry correct but no argument would prevail: I must wait until a telegram was sent to Juarez requesting verification of my personal legal entry. So back to Tapachula I stormed, re-registered at the hotel and sought liquids cooling to mind and body.

A few hours later Charley Walker parked on an adjacent bar stool. He had been in Tapachula for several years exporting livestock, had a room in the hotel and more impressive troubles than I. His local girl friend had missed her period and Charley knew his stateside wife

was not likely to be sympathetic. With nothing else to do we decided that a nice motorcycle ride might help. The girl friend borrowed a pair of slacks and we took off for the roughest ride I could find. It worked and by the next day she was back on schedule. Charley was so grateful for such assistance that he made it possible for me to meet many of the uniques in Tapachula where the daily paper listed 26 murders in the past month. An editorial in the same issue denounced the mayor for permitting members of the police department to throw a wild party in the town's best whore house. "It was formerly for respectable men," so the paper claimed.

One afternoon Charley introduced a truly lovely girl he said was only 12 years old. Her body was exquisite, the features regular and skin free from blemishes. I suggested that she would be a prize catch for some village boy but my opinion was far wrong. Some weeks previously the girl had remained away from home all night. When she returned the next morning she presented her father with $50. He asked where the money came from and she told him that one of the rich boys had paid for spending her first night with him. As Charley's story went, the father was so angry he pulled her pants down and whipped so hard she couldn't sit for two days. He had hoped for better things for his beautiful daughter and now that she was ruined, he was certain no decent man would marry her.

I made several trips to Talisman before a telegram finally arrived from Juarez. It made matters worse by reporting that I was in the country *ilegalda* (illegally) while the motorcycle was in the country *legalda* (legally).

There are 21 soldiers on this box car and 21 convicted murderers inside. I was told that if his prisoner escaped the responsible soldier would get to take the prisoner's place.

Accordingly I was to wait until the Mexican government issued a special exit permit, which could take as long as three weeks. On return to town a radio-telephone call was made to the U.S. Embassy in Mexico City. A most delicious female southern drawl was comforting but discouraging. She told me "You will have to wait two to three weeks for clearance." Charley was sympathetic and talked with some of his friends but they were powerless, as the officer holding me, *El Agente Auxiliar de la Jefatura Alberto Fernandez Colina*, was brand new and taking his job much too seriously.

Later, while on our way to the plaza for beers, Charley grabbed my arm, shouted "Stop!" and pulled me off the sidewalk. He had noticed, and I had not, a fine spray of water from the space between a partially open door and its frame. From inside the house a small boy had poked his weenie through the crack and was urinating without regard for who might be walking past his front door. We detoured and arrived safely at a kiosk table where several of Charley's locals waited to cadge a free beer.

In English, Charley told me that one of them was known to have disposed of three non-friends in the past two years. A few minutes later I was cautiously listening to the young man's dissertation on the value of a sharpened screwdriver in close combat while the instrument in question was waving under my overlong nose. The tricky part of carrying it in your pocket had been solved by a large cork stuck on the screwdriver's tip with a length of string tied from cork to belt loop. The cork kept the point from piercing the pocket and the cord pulled the cork off when emergency action appeared imminent. As a demonstration of effectiveness the screwdriver was driven into the table and completely pierced its inch-thick wooden top.

This peep show for children was near the marketplace in Tapachula. One show was about the Mexican revolution, another depicted Japan's attack on Hawaii and the third pictured a story of Cortes' Tree of the Sad Night.

I changed the subject and the youth with the screwdriver began to discuss wages and money. To demonstrate his point the young man displayed a matchstick and said it represented one U.S. dollar. By breaking off tiny bits of the wood he thoroughly expressed the long time required for a Mexican to earn equal money.

Later that evening Charley decided I needed a night out so he and his girl friend walked me through a back street to a small cantina. Carmen was the bartender's name, the cantina was owned by her father and she had no objection to closing the door after Charley told her that we would be there for a while. From Carmen I learned about two kinds of Mexican beer. Both bottles were priced the same but the one for tourists and drunks had three blue stars on the label. The other carried four stars, was more potent and was sold to friends. After a few four-stars Charley's girl friend began fighting with him and moved to sit with me in a futile attempt to promote a bit of conflict. I quietly left.

One day the hotel barkeeper found me checking the bike and asked questions about cost and riding techniques. My offer of a free trip was eagerly accepted. With noisy advice from his friends to "hang on" we stormed up the street at 50 miles an hour, leaned a corner, barely missed a goggled-eye policeman and streaked down the highway as rapidly as traffic permitted. During the return trip we boondocked along a randomly cobblestoned street where the bartender almost came unglued from the shocks of leaping from bump to bump. We coasted into the hotel patio 15 minutes later. He was weak from excitement and abandoned the fender on wobbly legs as his waiting friends made caustic comments about his bravery. One young man grabbed the bartender's crotch then recommended a change of underwear.

The three boys were happy to show me
this marvelous Mayan (?) work hidden in the
Chiapas jungles near the border river with Guatemala.

Suddenly they heard noises in the underbrush but decided they were of no importance and led me to even more interesting ruins.

I had been told of so-called Mayan ruins that had been ignored by archaeologists and government museum officers. This bit of information led to my being guided through jungle underbrush by three small boys. Only traces of a path were visible but they knew exactly where we were going. After a half-hour hike from the highway the oldest boy stopped and pointed ahead. I saw nothing but a small rise behind which was a larger mound of undergrowth. By circling both I found four elaborately carved rock slabs equally spaced around the large mound. The slabs were overgrown with weeds and surrounded by tall grass but after we cleaned the debris away we could see a variety of figures on the top and edges of each slab.

The boys took me about 100 yards farther from the high mound, cleared away more underbrush and showed me an an eight-foot-high carving that appeared to be either a snake or monkey's head. The jaws were stretched wide and between them was an unrecognizable figure. While I took pictures the boys peered off into the jungle but after a bit of discussion led me farther into the undergrowth to a low mound about 20 feet high and 140 feet in diameter. They said a woodcutter living nearby had told them it was the king's grave. It could have been. On one side were three slab rocks similar to our cemetery grave markers. The most visible of the group was a four-by six-foot plate carved to resemble a toad lying flat on the ground. Behind it, nearer the mound, was a standing headpiece about three feet wide by fourteen feet tall which was intricately carved with symbols and designs of the most obscure meaning.

While I inspected these amazing works the boys talked nervously among themselves. Finally thc eldest approached and said, "We must go now." From the urgency in his voice I didn't argue. We hiked only a short distance before the cause of their alarm became obvious. Indians were silently gliding through the jungle on both sides of us to be certain we left their sacred area promptly. Discovery of the escorts increased our strides and soon the four of us were back on the highway, I with not enough pictures in the camera and the boys with well-earned pesos in hand.

Several nights later Charley and his girl invited me to visit her 9-by 12-foot rented room for which Charley was paying Mex. $30 ($4.U.S.) a month. As I was curious about the housing of a poor Mexican woman, the invitation was accepted and I arrived eager-eyed. First they introduced me to cousins, friends and the inevitable sister. Then served a cool beer for all except the 14-year-old living next door who was nursing her fatherless child. I was given one of two chairs while Charley and his friend sat on their bed of planks stretched between two low sawhorses. The top of the bed was covered by a light cotton blanket under a purple bedspread. An old cardboard suitcase showed under the planks. Two clean dresses sagged on nails and a douche bag hung above the head of the bed.

The room's whitewashed walls were decorated with colorful calendar prints and cigarette advertisements A solitary table held our beer bottles. The light source was one candle stuck onto a small charcoal stove made from stones stacked on an old apple box. There were two small shelves, one an altar with its perpetual candle burning dimly amid fresh ferns and another which supported a small amount of foodstuffs. A few dishes and eating utensils

Each time the odometer rolled over to X000 I took a picture. This is at 4000 miles, on the Tapachula-Talisman road. Nearby hills are in Guatemala.

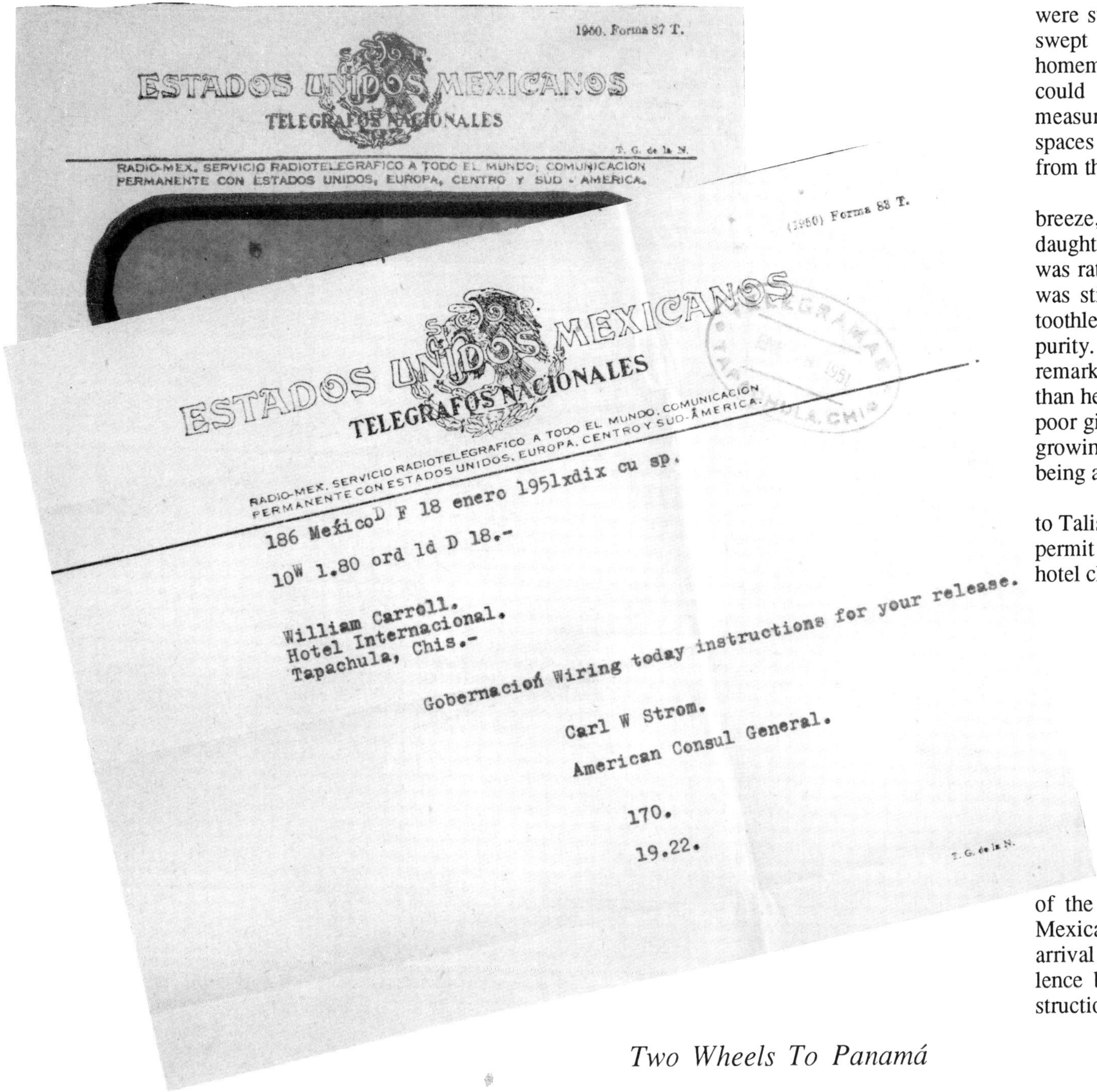
1950. Forma 87 T.

ESTADOS UNIDOS MEXICANOS

TELEGRAFOS NACIONALES

T. G. de la N.

RADIO-MEX. SERVICIO RADIOTELEGRAFICO A TODO EL MUNDO; COMUNICACION PERMANENTE CON ESTADOS UNIDOS, EUROPA, CENTRO Y SUD - AMERICA.

(1950) Forma 83 T.

ESTADOS UNIDOS MEXICANOS

TELEGRAFOS NACIONALES

RADIO-MEX. SERVICIO RADIOTELEGRAFICO A TODO EL MUNDO. COMUNICACION PERMANENTE CON ESTADOS UNIDOS, EUROPA, CENTRO Y SUD-AMERICA.

186 Mexico D F 18 enero 1951xdix cu sp.

10W 1.80 ord ld D 18.-

William Carroll.
Hotel Internacional.
Tapachula, Chis.-

Gobernación Wiring today instructions for your release.

Carl W Strom.

American Consul General.

170.

19.22.

T. G. de la N.

were stacked on a board raised above the well-swept dirt floor by several large rocks. The homemade wood door sagged to the floor but could be barred after closing to provide a measure of security. Ventilation was through spaces where the tin roof missed the walls and from the now open doorway.

While we were cooling from a passing breeze, the landlady brought her 16-year-old daughter over to be introduced to me. The girl was rather unattractive and Charley asked if she was still a virgin. Her face lit up with a huge toothless smile as she acknowledged her pristine purity. Not being able to keep a straight face I remarked that it was good she could run faster than her brothers. For the rest of the evening the poor girl's life was miserable from teasing about growing to 16 and retaining her virginity by being able to run fast.

During the idle days I made daily trips to Talisman in hopes that word would arrive and permit me to leave Mexico. One morning the hotel clerk gave me a telegram.

I thought I was free at last to check out of the hotel, say farewell to Charley and my Mexican friends then head to the border. But my arrival at Talisman was greeted with dead silence by Colina. He had received no such instructions and would not release me.

A Mexican friend decided I needed a traveling companion and offered to give me Chungo. He was a friendly little beast but not at all happy on the noisy bike.

Colina said there was no telephone communication with his superior in Nuevo Suchiate 20 miles away so I carried my telegram and a letter from Colina over on the motorcycle. The chief said he was sorry but he had no order to release me. After he read the Consul's telegram a second time, I understood him to say he would write a letter to the Talisman station telling them I could cross the border. He wrote a letter and I delivered it, only to learn it stated "Hold this man until our government permits his release." I was dumbfounded but telling Colina what I though of such collective stubbornness would have helped not at all. After the day of run-around, I sadly rode back to Tapachula and the Hotel Internacional.

This continuing delay was bending the daily budget out of shape so the next day I checked into the less expensive Hotel Imperial on a day-to-day basis. It was a two-storey wooden structure with about 50 rooms facing a patio loaded with birds that persisted in singing the sun up and the guests out, early. My room was finished in colonial antiquity with peeling plaster, a very short iron bed with a thin pad over woven ropes, and towels so thin I dried on the last person to use them. As I am over six feet tall it was easy to be certain of remaining in bed all night. All I had to do was slide my feet between rails at the foot of the bed and wedge my head against bars at the other end. It sounds uncomfortable but after one falls asleep in that fashion it is complete protection against nocturnal earthquakes, floors that might collapse during the night or rolling out of bed.

One day at Talisman I met a Mexican air force captain on vacation. At least that is what he said. This elegantly uniformed airman approached and inquired about the trouble I was having at the border. I went over the difficulties in detail and he disappeared for a few minutes. Soon he was back and asked, "How much money do you have?" I didn't think that was much of his business and gave a rather nebulous reply. The nonsense must have been impressive as he then went into his sales' pitch.

I was confidentially told that my new "friend" was the Mexican president's private pilot and here was his pilot's log book as proof. He was leaving for Mexico City that afternoon and for 1000 pesos ($12 U.S.) he would bring back my exit permit within two days. This sounded too good to be true. Or should I admit it smelled. I wasn't interested but the man would not give up. I was still saying "No" 30 minutes later when he piled into his car, equipped with a dandy blonde, and drove off into Guatemala.

In town that evening I mentioned the incident to a Mexican businessman and the rest of the story came out. The so-called officer had arrived in Tapachula several days before and by using his uniform and pilot log book as identification had charged merchandise in nearly every store in town. On the same morning he met me at the border one of the merchants became suspicious and called the police. The fly-boy must have had friends because a few minutes after the police were notified he left town with the girl friend.

In an attempt to move Mexican officialdom at a pace more rapid than dormant I decided to spend each day at Talisman until they finally released me. This was bad news for Colina because I soon learned that the other border officers were more friendly. Each one personally apologized for Colina's stupidity, explained that he was making a huge mistake, they could do nothing but sincerely hoped I would not judge all Mexican officials in the light of this senseless experience.

My first full day was highlighted after the border bridge was closed for lunch, which it was from noon until two every day. A recent truckload of liquor had crossed the line and the driver had donated several liters of brandy to the Talisman staff. As soon as the bridge chain went up we trooped into Talisman's small cafe, which was nothing more than a two-room wooden shack. One room contained beds, a beverage cooler without ice and a small stock of canned goods. The other room contained two rickety tables surrounded by benches and chairs for patrons. There was a screened cupboard for dishes and an uncovered fire in one corner for cooking. The only window did double duty as a source of ventilation and for garbage disposal to dogs waiting outside. Keeping the cafe floor clean was managed by chickens who seemed always underfoot but were never stepped on. Meanwhile a collection of shoeless children wandered in and out to swipe tortillas from the stack being heated for lunch. Because the tables were surrounded by hungry people, and there was no other relatively flat surface available, one of the cooks had her skirt high and was flattening fresh tortilla dough on her bare thigh.

Pre-lunch brandy enhanced our satisfaction with the chicken and rice after which we turned our attention to serious testing of the gift liquor. Except Colina, everyone from the post collected at least a short water glass or two. The officers repeatedly told me they did not like him and had expressly not asked him to join the group. With this in mind, after lunch I lurched into his somewhat plush office, stretched out on the sofa and went to sleep. Three hours later Talisman's secretary woke me and explained that no word had been received and as all the day's communications were in I should go back to town. Back and forth continued for a few more days minus either gift liquor or communication from the Mexican government. On the upbeat side, the border officers were good company and Colina had become increasingly upset.

On Saturday the 22nd another tragedy seemed to be in the making.

That afternoon my return to the Hotel Imperial was marked with a strange lack of enthusiasm when I rode into the lobby as usual. The owner was cornered and the bad news was bad indeed. She had already rented every room and there was no place for me to sleep. My unhappy comments were not too polite but at least she got the idea, felt sorry for me and produced a towel so I could shower before dinner.

After the meal was over by an hour or so she asked if I would mind sleeping in the maid's room. A few minutes later the maid led me to the hotel's farthest back room next to the kitchen. Through the open door I saw three beds, a small trunk, the usual burning altar candle and a shelf of cosmetics. The maid showed me which bed was mine and left. I dumped my clothes on a chair, turned the light off and stretched my overlong frame along the sagging mattress. Though I had vowed to remain awake until the maid arrived, all of a sudden there was sunlight in the room and kitchen noises were beating on my ears. The maid's bed was as pure and untouched as my emotions. Breakfast was a dreary meal relieved by the hotel owner asking how I slept. Rather sourly I replied that I had "slept" all night.

My arrival at Talisman was unusual in that very few officers were in sight. I wandered through the building until I found the rest of the staff huddled around the solitary telephone. My entrance was the signal for an explosion of Spanish. A telegram was being telephoned through and I was released. Additional news was that the first telegram from Juarez had contained a typographical error. The word *legalda* (legal) had been sent originally as meaning I had entered the country legally. However during transcription an "*i*" had been inserted creating the word *ilegalda* (illegal). The anticlimax was even more disheartening. The senior officer showed me a letter that Colina had received two weeks before that instructed him to pass me through the border upon payment of a Mex. $25 ($3 U.S.) bond. Colina, unhappy with Americans or Carroll or whatever, had not shown me the letter and apparently thought it safe to hide it. No one else had seen the letter arrive but the Talisman secretary found it while retrieving my passport from Colina's files because he was absent on his day off.

(Colina was gone when I passed through Talisman two years later. Many officers remembered me and we enjoyed another border-closing party in the tiny cafe.)

They prepared a new tourist card and stamped my passport. I paid Mex. $3 (35¢ U.S.), took a picture of all the officers to better remember them in my will and rode over the bridge into Guatemala. The Guatemalan officers were pleasant, had known about my troubles and were ready to pass me through. But a hitch developed. I had been detained in Mexico so long that my Guatemalan entry visa had expired. Nothing would do but I should hustle back to Tapachula for another visa. I returned over the Suchiate bridge, was passed into Mexico without formality and headed for town to find the Guatemalan consulate office.

I managed to impress the consul with urgency of the situation, obtained a visa stamp in several minutes and started back to Talisman. It was past noon and from days of practically living there I knew the border would be chained closed for two hours. Twelve to two. This time it was different. The Mexican officers had delayed closing the border, waved me past without hesitation then locked the barrier chain as I coasted into Guatemala.

Estados Unidos Mexicanos
Secretaria de Gobernacioñ
Salida...Ene 23 1951...Talisman...Chis.

(Passport stamp.)

The entire Talisman staff stopped traffic and work so I could take this most informal picture before leaving Mexico and entering Guatemala.

Talisman Frontera...Guatemala C.A
Ingresso...23 Ene 1951

On the Guatemalan side two officers were waiting. As I rolled over the Suchiate bridge they unlocked the chain on their side, passed me without inspection, opened the registry kiosk, stamped me into the country and wished me a pleasant visit. It had taken three weeks to cross a simple 75-foot international bridge.

It was nearly one o'clock and finally I was bumping along the dirt and gravel beginning of Guatemala's *Ruta 1*, their section of *La Carretera Interamericana*. The roadway wandered through a jungle of dense growth and infrequent bamboo huts for a few miles, into a winding river canyon, then headed up into the mountains. It was wide enough for two cars and presented no problem other than being rough.

Eleven miles from the border I reached the village of Malacatán where the only hotel was also the only place to eat. I warned a half-dozen kids to leave the bike alone and ordered lunch after washing up at the community wash bowl. Food was so long overdue that my stomach began to worry. In the kitchen, which was a wooden shed leaning against the backside of a ragged fence, three cooks were watching my hostess struggle with a broken can opener. With their approval my scout knife opened enough cans to feed an army. Verbal tokens of appreciation were expressed and a few minutes later my first Guatemalan meal stared me in the face: good soup, salad, steak, fried potatoes and rice. For desert they served a peeled orange

This stone bridge in the tropic lowlands was dedicated July 19, 1881. "Justice" has been defaced on the original inscription which was "Liberty and Justice".

A temporary wooden crossing covered the old ford
for this small river while a new one-lane steel
structure was erected as time and funds became available.

impaled on a fork. In paying for the meal, another surprise was in store. Guatemala currency, the *quetzal*, was on a par with that of the States and 65 cents made lunch a bargain.

With my stomach cared for and gasoline inspected we left Malacatán toward the planned overnight in the mountain town of La Unión. From lunch onward the miles were progressively more difficult as *Ruta 1* became a narrow pair of one-way ruts. Slopes were often so steep that when forward motion was canceled to take pictures it was necessary to foot-push or restart diagonally across the tracks. In more scenic areas the route had been notched into the solid rock mountainsides before it would drop into tiny valleys to cross temporary wooden bridges or give me more practice at fording streams. When the rare car or truck approached I stopped on what shoulder was available so it could pass.

The further the higher and within an hour tropical heat became only a pleasant memory as chill mountain air frosted my bones. I quickly passed through a few villages, although in one a policeman recorded my name, license number and destination. The ruts led higher and by the time I was 35 miles from the border my glasses were fogging from low clouds and a fine mist dripped off my face and clothes. At *Ruta 1's* highest point a sign advised me that it was 9015 feet above sea level. This was also the beginning of a wider and better roadway leading down to the valley of San Marcos and a police booth (4340 miles) where I registered my name and license plate number.

I had been sent to the Hotel Longo, in La Unión, which turned out to be an excellent recommendation. Lodging was Q2.50 ($2.50 U.S.) including dinner and breakfast. It was comfortable though there was no running water because the town's utility service had not repaired a broken pipe and the community's water was wandering along the main street. The hotel's owner, a Sr. Perez, had arrived from Spain with his wife and children eleven years before. They did their best to make me feel at home and tuned a short-wave radio in the dining room so I could hear an American news broadcast from New York. After dinner they invited the town's only physician in for coffee and to tell me something about his work. Dr. Eduardo Chang, who had been educated in both the United States and Guatemala, was in charge of a 50-bed public hospital recently built in La Unión. We had a great time discussing our countries, amateur motion pictures and the Korean war. It was with regret that I parted from my host and his guest and went to bed, which was totally different from the night before. In Tapachula it had been so hot that I threw off the light sheet. In La Unión I slept well under a pile of coarse blankets which appeared locally made.

Perez woke me in the morning and left a pitcher of warm water for shaving and washing. Breakfast was served by an elderly Indian waiter who proudly told me he had worked at the hotel 14 years. He wore a coat and vest for protection against the morning chill but padded on bare feet between the kitchen and my table. Gasoline at the town's only station was 50 *centavos* (50¢ U.S.) a gallon hand-pumped from a 55-gallon drum. The two-gallon fill-up caused envious comments from bystanders owning automobiles.

This twisting roadway in the tropic lowlands was often bordered by these unusual barriers. In the highlands, where cliffs were higher, there were no barriers.

The road from here to Quezaltenango was somewhat better though it too was notched into mountain sides and wandered through cultivated valleys. Quezaltenango was a somewhat modern town with block-paved streets, taxi cabs and neon signs. Red flags hung from many buildings and hundreds of people loitered on the sidewalks. I had no reason to stop and departed on a dirt road several degrees worse than the one that had brought me into town.

Strangely enough, every few miles there was a policeman, all spit and polish, standing by the side of the road. I was certain they weren't looking for me and kept moving. Several small villages on this section of *Ruta 1* were also decorated with red flags and townspeople were on door steps or by the road. Police huddled at intersections as though a parade was expected and a few miles further on the parade found me. While I was coping with the winding mountain road, a huge black Cadillac limousine lumbered past, spraying dust in my face and over the countryside. A man in the back seat waved as though apologizing for the inconvenience. Following it was an open Dodge roadster with three military officers in the rear seat. They were so covered with dust it was impossible to decide where faces began and uniforms left off. I gave everyone a thorough cursing, brushed myself off and poked along farther. As I second-geared up a long slope more vehicles appeared over the crest. They were lead by jeeps crammed with armed soldiers, followed by several Cadillac sedans, two new Mercuries, a fleet of new Packards, and two more jeeps of soldiers bringing up the rear. Several hundred yards behind their dust cloud I saw a young man riding a Triumph.

The small red flag next to the street light pictures the newly elected President of Guatemala and announces that he will visit the town during the next day.

Keith Barrow had dropped his Triumph once and was still having trouble with the dirt and rocks of Guatemala's roadway.

He stopped and introduced himself as Keith Barrow of Oakland, California. Keith had been working in Arabian oil fields and saved his pay to tour Central America on the way home. And there was a question. "How do you keep this damn motorcycle from sliding around in the dirt?" he asked. He had never ridden until buying the new Triumph in Nicaragua three weeks before. The 1100 miles on its odometer were his total experience and he had not been too happy with the handling problems of thick dust and ruts of *Ruta 1*. We talked about dirt riding, took pictures of each other and he explained the parade of guards and Cadillacs. Guatemala had recently elected a new president who was now touring to thank his constituents for their votes and seek their ongoing support.

I continued through more mountain ranges and an increasing number of villages. By late afternoon there were a few road construction projects, the miles became easier and *Ruta 1* spewed me forth onto a wide asphalt highway.

This 20 miles of completed *La Carretera Interamericana* was smooth sailing at fifty miles an hour over a beautiful mountain pass with scenic views at every curve. It was so wonderful I almost stopped to kiss the black stuff but decided it would be more satisfying to continue into Guatemala City for a warm shower. By the time I arrived (4519 miles) it had taken nine solid hours to travel 165 miles, the final 20 of which had been paved. As expected, I wasted a little time being lost before a Cooks Tours' office pointed my wheels toward the *Palacio Nacional* where the guards wore Hollywood-style cream and red, or black and red, uniforms. One guard led me to the National Tourist Bureau office for mail and the address of a pension for my planned two-week visit to *La República de Guatemala*.

This was the Interamerican Highway leading to Guatemala City from the Mexican border by Tapachula. It was all similar dirt except for the last 20 miles.

The mail was pleasant and the pension address only a short ride to a large red stone house with an eight-foot-high carved entry door. An Indian maid answered the bell then called her mistress who showed up in a dressing gown at 4:30 in the afternoon. About 5'5", 125 pounds, big brown eyes, lustrous dark hair and a million dollars worth of smile, she was a widow who took borders to make ends meet. I wasted no time accepting her hospitality and helped move a double bed into my room. Dinner was served in the patio immediately following my first hot tub bath in nearly a month.

After a few days of touristing the city I rode to Santo Thomás Chichicastenango, which is the often-photographed town with a church known for local Indians burning incense on the front steps. The Indians believe that smoke of the incense carries their prayers directly to heaven. The town's tourist hotel offered super-deluxe accommodations at the super-deluxe price of Q15 ($15 U.S.) a night. Two blocks away the commercial hotel provided excellent meals and a comfortable room with a fireplace in the corner for Q3 ($3 U.S.) a night.

While I was wandering around Chichicastenango on Saturday, a crippled boy, swinging on a crude crutch, introduced himself as Sebastian Ponjoy and said he would be glad to show me around as my time permitted. A fee was agreed and Sebastian hired. He decided that first I must see their shrine atop a nearby mountain that I had heard was most interesting. It took an hour-long hike into a pine forest before we reached a cleared area, which contained four stone objects decorated with fresh flowers.

The famous Chichicastenango church contains no pews. Inside, the entire stone floor is literally covered with burning candles. Three Indians are praying by the door.

The cross and Mayan (?) figure are left of Sebastian. Behind him, on the right, the low brush shelter covers two more small crosses. Incense burned on the rock in front.

One was a Christian-like cross about a foot high. Next to it was a crude Mayan or Indian figure that was about three feet high. After I took a few still pictures we waited until I was able to shoot motion pictures of an Indian family on their way to town. They stopped to burn incense while praying to Christian and Pagan gods at the same time, a unique way of making prayer doubly effective.

Sebastian explained that fresh flower offerings were always made prior to beginning any important endeavor. White blossoms were a silent prayer for long life and much happiness. Pink flowers were considered a gesture of appreciation for good crops. Yellow eased the lot of relatives long since dead. Red aided in successful business deals. And green flowers, plus prayer, would (hopefully) cause rain, he said.

Because marriages were often solemnized before the two images, Sebastian gave me a detailed description of the custom. Most important, he said, was that family happiness was based on practical selection instead of beauty. By the time a boy reached the age of ten or twelve his father usually had decided on a prospective bride whose parents possessed some form of wealth. On a Sunday evening the matchmaking father and his son would load themselves with gifts of food, liquor, cigars, sweets and cloth then go to the home of the intended bride. A knock at the door was sufficient greeting. If they were invited to enter the deal was nearly clinched. However, should the girl's father call though the door "My daughter is to be married soon" then matchmaking father, son and gifts would depart. Because the betrothal was so often arranged beforehand, the traditional Sunday door-knocking was more to party and for the bride to meet her future husband.

Most ceremonies were held at the hilltop retreat because church weddings were so costly there would be little money left for a subsequent celebration. Sexual relations were not permitted during the "engagement" though the couple usually waited until the boy was between 16 and 20 before marriage. After a complicated two-hour marriage ritual a rooster, which had been brought by the groom, would be decapitated with one swing of the Shaman's machete. The headless animal was freed to flop and bleed because the longer it remained active the longer would be the groom's life. Next a hen, provided by the bride, was similarly dealt with and from actions of her bird were read other important phases of their married life. If the hen lived as long as the rooster had, and was as active, the new couple were suited to each other. However if the hen lived longer than the rooster the husband would have a short life or, if not as long, the bride would die young. Should the hen be more active than the rooster her husband will not be sufficiently eager in the bedroom and if the opposite occurs the groom should maintain a few female friends.

After both fowl were dead the marriage party would pray for a few minutes to their Christian and Pagan gods then go to the groom's house for a blowout hosted by the bride's parents. The party could last from a few hours to a week depending on how much money there was to spend. When hangovers had disappeared the bride moved into the home of the groom's parents where she was taught wifely duties of cooking, child care and weaving, the latter to earn money towards her own home. When two relatively wealthy families intermarried, the parents often gave the new family a small plot of land to farm and built them a new house. Otherwise the groom worked in the fields for several years, while saving every *centavo* to move his wife and children into their own home. In this he would be helped by both sets of parents. The moving of a new family into their home would be the occasion of another celebration including practical gifts such as cloth, candles or livestock. Because the Indians did not trust paper money their cash donations were traditionally made with Guatemala's largest coin, the *quetzal 25 centavo* piece.

It was cold in Chichicastenango that evening when I wandered around. On the church steps two Indians waved tins of smoking incense and prayed loudly while nearby a town boy lit a cigarette and cast a momentary yellow halo around the devout Indian faces. From the dark of a side street, voices mingled with the creak of back-racks loaded with stock for tomorrow's market. I could see carpenters assembling wooden chairs by candlelight while a family of six threaded their way toward the church steps. Here they unharnessed shoulder racks of clay pots so the children could light long candles from others already burning. They tilted the

new candles, one for each family member, to drip wax, which would hold them upright on steps nearest the doorway. The family had walked many a mile with cargo on their back but considered it important to pray before finding a place to sleep in the crowded marketplace.

Along one side of the central plaza a long covered porch protected groups of market folk huddled around fires while cooking their evening meal, singing quietly and drinking. The cold kept them close and a newcomer would have had trouble approaching the pot for something to eat. In the center of the plaza the single dim light bulb illuminated a splash of color on the bandstand. I moved closer and found five sleeping Indians sprawled under varicolored blankets. On the other side of the plaza was another covered porch. There were no cooking fires, only row on row of bodies sleeping on straw mats with goods for tomorrow's market stacked between the owner and wall.

That night, being a cautious character, I locked my bedroom door but when breakfast time arrived it could not be unlocked. My pocket-knife screwdriver undid the hinges to get the door off and dismantle the lock so its six-inch long key could be removed.

The market on Sunday included dozens of tourists mixing it up with centuries-old Guatemalan customs. And the Indians were nobody's fool. To take pictures from the roof of a nearby building I had to find the boy with the ladder concession. He would let me use the ladder "borrowed from the mayor" and could I leave him a small tip for his trouble. Business was good for there must have been at least twenty people on the roof during the morning.

Orderly confusion is the keynote of most native markets and this was no exception. Pots and pans were mixed with clothing and

The market scene was changing dramatically and here most men are dressed in modern clothing while the women wear their traditional hand-woven garments.

foods were stacked next to livestock. A fine coffin sold for Q3 ($3 U.S.), a hand-painted chair for 40 *centavos* (40¢ U.S.), a large carved chest for Q4 ($4 U.S.), 12-inch clay pots for ten *centavos* each, a big lunch for eight and small supper for five. Meals for small fry were free. One rather elderly-appearing woman had swung a sagging breast back under her armpit to nurse the baby strapped on her back. Behind her a drunk lying on the ground was kicking at a woman trying to move him out of the sun. The conglomeration of sights was enough to keep a camera busy for months but the best shots were often missed. Such as the Indian girl dressed in lovely hand-woven native clothes, wearing exquisite filigree jewelry and carrying her baby in a colorful native shoulder pouch. In contrast, the baby had on a store-bought knitted jacket and wore a green and orange baseball cap.

The following morning, before I departed on the 120-mile ride back to Guatemala City, I had to inspect an already perfectly functioning spark plug and break the porcelain by being careless with the plug wrench. Spares were at my Guatemala City pension. The local druggist (who also served as the town doctor) owned a pre-war Royal Enfield but he had no spare plugs. A friend was sent to find something and returned with two super-size jobs from a Model A Ford. By this time a number of vice-presidents had collected, one of whom knew a man with an automobile. A group of about a dozen Indians led me to this poor man's house and no doubt scared him half to death with their hammering on the front door. He gave me a plug that fit the hole, much to my relief.

Antigua, an early capital of Guatemala, was a most interesting site with its multitude of ruined structures retaining evidence of their original character.

These handsome masks were but two of about 20 contained in impressive antique chests. They were used during annual ceremonies and never left the village.

Antigua, the nation's fourth capital city which was destroyed by the earthquakes of 1717 and 1773, was not too far from Guatemala city.

When I was in Antigua the site was a wondrous collection of demolished churches, monasteries and civic buildings, most of which had not been restored. A friend had sent me to the parish priest who knew of Indians treasuring centuries-old wooden masks used for their traditional ceremonies. The priest convinced a village lad to ride on the back of the BSA and guide me along a bewildering maze of jungle footpaths to a collection of bamboo huts nearly an hour away. The lad's introduction to the headman, as requested by the priest, was enough. A pair of marvelous wooden chests of indeterminate antiquity were opened by the headman's daughter and I was handling treasures that were never allowed to leave the village. The wooden masks had been used so often that the insides were worn smooth where they rested on the wearers' faces. I couldn't determine if they had been repainted but the exteriors were fearsomely realistic. After taking pictures I was invited to share a simple fare of tortillas, eggs and beans served to me on an upturned apple-box while the headman's family sat on the dirt floor to eat.

One of my more peculiar experiences occurred in Guatemala City. One day in the central park I chanced on an opportunity to photograph the Metropolitan Cathedral in its best light. To decide how to best compose the picture the cathedral and fountain were framed from several locations between my hands. As I lowered my outstretched arms for the last time the fountain spray diminished to a trickle. This caused me no concern but on turning toward the camera I noticed a back-country Indian family of three staring open-mouthed. The old man approached, pointed to the now dormant fountain, touched my arms and said something that I interpreted as "How did you turn it down?"

For once my wits were equal to the occasion. I replied in simple Spanish, "Yes, I did it. It is nothing" and began taking pictures. What a story he must have told his village friends about the tall *ladino* (non-Indian white) who controlled water with a wave of his hands.

One pleasantly warm evening several days later I broke the sad news of imminent departure to my charming landlady. Her sorrow at such parting was amply demonstrated and I had the devil's own time kicking the motorcycle to life the next morning. Besides being sleepy I was dumbed out, misunderstood a policeman's instructions and left Guatemala City (5231 miles) on the wrong road to El Salvador. There were two highways toward the south, one of which was wide, well-graded and untraveled because it didn't go anywhere, as I soon learned. I back-tracked to the other, which was the completely unsurfaced, rough-as-a-cob, *La Carretera Interamericana.*

After thumping along for about 20 miles I paid through the nose for traveling too fast over such territory. A rear fender brace broke, dropped my cargo on the tire and effectively halted forward motion. Whittling branches from a nearby tree and making repairs wasn't difficult. But long underwear donned for the cold highland morning gave me a hot time in the tropic lowlands. After the brace was strapped in place I rode more slowly. It took no adding machine to count traffic. After leaving the capital city I saw only three busses, two jeeps and two passenger cars all the way to the Guatemalan frontier with El Salvador.

The presidential palace and Cathedral of Guatemala City faced toward this fountain in the central square.

They were still working on this section of the Interamerican Highway when I passed through about two years later. Little had changed.

My plentiful supply of wooden braces was essential until I managed to cut one to the exact length to hold fender and cargo above the rear tire.

When I reached the frontier I had to pass through a small village to enter the Guatemalan control station. I motored onto the concrete inspection apron but no one was in sight. The engine must have awakened the post as several officers were rubbing sleepy eyes when they appeared. Paperwork was all in order and the rubber stamp well dried in my passport when I was turned over to the *aduanero* who wanted to inspect my cargo. To be friendly I took his picture sitting on the cycle before he told me I must pay him Q2.75 ($2.75 U.S.).

This bad news completely destroyed my modest command of Spanish and for some reason or another I couldn't understand what he wanted except for the Q2.75. I explained in English that they had charged me to enter their country, I had paid the consul for a visa to leave, the government had charged me to import my own film and it wasn't legal to charge me just to pass his border. The poor guard went through his act again by writing Q2.75 on a piece of paper and told me that because it was Sunday he was permitted to charge extra, it was a legal fee and would I please pay up and leave for El Salvador. I couldn't understand this either so we settled for a 25 *centavo* (25¢ U.S.) stamp for the passport. He appeared to have been a little upset because the office door was slammed in the faces of his laughing fellow guards as he retreated to his desk.

Salida de Guatemala...San Cristóbal...Frontera Guatemala, C.A....11 Feb 1951

Even after I took his picture atop the BSA, the customs officer insisted that I pay a "Sunday" fee for his services while leaving Guatemala.

Delegacion de Migracion
San Cristobal Frontera
Entro de Fecha 11 Feb 1951

Modern downtown San Salvador showed bicycles and motocycles as a common mode of transportation. The large stores displayed broad selections of merchandise.

The 200 feet into El Salvador began through a wire gate onto pavement leading to a neat little border office where well-dressed officers spoke a little English and presented a cordial reception to this tourist and one dirty motorcycle. After details were completed and fees paid I was directed to an adjoining lunchroom where the counterman handed me a chilled cola and list of sandwiches. Cheese between fresh bread and the cold drink at 75 *centavos* (35¢ U.S.) were great after 105 dusty miles of rough dirt. Because the main roads in El Salvador were paved the next nine miles to an *aduana* (customs) station at Candelaria took exactly eleven minutes. Inspection included officers checking my passport and the bike's VIN number before attaching a metal seal to match the BSA's serially-numbered import certificate. From there to San Salvador, the capital, was a hurried 90 miles because the sun was low on the horizon.

While thumping down San Salvador's main boulevard (5554 miles) I was on the right side of a bus when a traffic cop pulled it over, during which operation the bus almost ran over me. Escape was past an unnoticed stop sign to the musical accompaniment of police whistles. My ears must have been dirty as I don't remember hearing whistles and did not want to participate in the bus driver's problem. A gasoline station attendant satisfied my need for guidance and pointed to the American Embassy a block away. Inside the open Embassy gate a young man in civilian clothes introduced himself as a U.S. Marine guard by the name of H.C. Smith.

The five community wash bowls of the San Salvador pension were always busy early in the morning which was a good excuse for me to sleep in and breakfast last.

Smith gave me a city map, a warning about one-way streets and sent me to the Pension Salvadoreña. I checked in at ₡6 *colones* ($2.40 U.S.) a day with meals. After showering the owner served dinner in a landscaped open patio where stones, painted to resemble green avocados, held the tablecloth from blowing away. Service was somewhat unique in that pre-served plates were brought to a sidebar, inspected by the host and then delivered to the guest's table. (The cook had raisins in the chicken dumplings. Good!)

At the pension I met Jim McClintock, an employee of the U.S. government, who walked me to a nearby pension to meet other Americans. They included Marines on Embassy guard duty, a railway consultant, store managers and a few tourists eager to hear about the bike trip. One of the Marines was organizing his marriage to a local woman the following week. Under El Salvador law he would first be married in a civil ceremony, which gave him a wife in name only. Three or four days later a church wedding would complete the joining and he could have the girl. Not complicated but, from his complaints, rough on the eager generation.

Bright and early my first morning I showered, shampooed, shaved and completed a daily action when a survey of the surroundings disclosed a complete lack of toilet tissue. A frantic search through my jumper pockets found only a piece of very solid U.S. Government printing, my income tax blank. So I did with my income tax blank what so many other taxpayers would like to do. And report that it is a very unsatisfactory substitute for the rolled material.

Next duty of the day was a trip to El Salvador's immigration bureau to obtain permission to stay in the country for a few weeks. The clerk told me "No photos of you, no permission," which called for a round-trip to the pension for additional pictures. The nearest bank exchanged traveler's checks for El Salvador currency at the rate of 2.50 *colones* for one dollar. McClintock had invited me to make use of the small garage where he supervised the service of U.S. vehicles. There the bike was drained and refilled, the broken bracket welded, engine tuned and everything steam cleaned.

My new friends had warned of the necessity for sharp bargaining so my mind was firmly set to pay as little as possible for 24-hour

(L to R) Berta, daughter of Donna Alvarengo who is the sister of Fr. Antonio, and Berta's sister Celina in front of the new church building in Santa Tecla.

Fr. Antonio's brother was the contractor for the Santa Tecla church. Half of the planned structure, behind the wooden partition, is completely finished and used daily.

parking space in a private garage across from the pension. The owner of the collection of sagging roofs known as Lopez Talleres looked me over and decided I would stand still for his highest rate of 25 *centavos* (10¢ U.S.) a day. I was much too sharp to accept his first offer and explained in my very best Spanish that I would pay only ₡2 (80 cents) a week. He quickly accepted. At dinner two hours later it finally dawned on me why the manager's very young son burst out laughing at the American who couldn't calculate a week's rent.

One of my pleasant obligations in El Salvador was to take a few photographs of the Los Angeles consul's brother. He was a priest in the small town of Santa Tecla, aka Nueva San Salvador, about nine miles southwest of the capital city. After a good breakfast I rode to the home of Father Antonio. He was so delighted to see someone from the States that he passed the word around and it seemed that half his parish came over to inspect me and the BSA. His church was only partially completed but behind its temporary facade the altar glowed with floral

Incoming sacks of cement were moved the hard way, one at a time on a stevedore's back. Coffee was being loaded on hoist platforms in the same manner.

contributions which softened the impact of a dozen rows of hard straight-back pews that would have kept the most sleepy parishioner awake. The townspeople were contributing labor, materials and what money they could spare. Fr. Antonio said that he laid the floor bricks in his spare time under direction of his brother who was acting as the contractor.

The priest's two nieces were attractive lasses of 18 and 24 who, while I was photographing Fr. Antonio, asked me to make pictures of them. I agreed and both women changed into their Sunday best. The younger girl, Celina, was the more friendly while the elder, Berta, was a bit shy. They invited me to join the family for lunch and I accepted without remorse. On the table they had soup, chicken, rice, steak, a leg of lamb, baked bananas, buns, soda pop, huge glasses of local wine and fresh fruit. Near the end of this huge meal Celina carefully peeled the biggest orange and presented it to me with a bright smile. Fr. Antonio told her that the other male guest, who was sulking somewhat like an unhappy suitor, had finished his meal and was ready for an orange whereas I was not. Celina smiled at me again and shrugged her shoulders at the good padre. Her sister saved the day by giving the young man an orange she had peeled. I had no desire to remain in Santa Tecla so excused myself a bit later and rode to the port of La Libertad.

The wharf was busy receiving sacks of cement and shipping coffee, which was El Salvador's most important export. After a few pictures I went back to San Salvador and stopped for gasoline at the Esso station that had been so helpful the day I arrived. The tank was filled while attendants and hangers-on plied me with questions. A city bus pulled in for water and the pump jockey shouted that I had ridden a motorcycle all the way from California. Transit schedules were forgotten as passengers and driver pushed out the door to inspect the two-wheeled machinery and its license plate. This time I had to say nothing as the service-station owner presented a complete and mostly erroneous version of my trip.

My padre of Santa Tecla had invited me to return the following Sunday to see a parish festival (*turno*) that he had organized to raise funds for completion of the new church. When I arrived the *turno* was a going business with many of the same devices used in the States. Their bingo game was well patronized and I found it more interesting than our urbanized activity. Because few older people could read, the cards displayed colored pictures of common objects: a melon, drunk, king, orange, automobile, horse or angel, for a total of 40 different subjects. The caller used a deck of cards with identical pictures. After shuffling he would very slowly turn the top card over, inspect it well

For a small coin the caged bird would select a personal fortune guaranteed to become true when supported by a church-building contribution.

and before the object was revealed make an obscure spiel about what it was. Sometimes the players out-guessed him and roared the answer before his announcement. At other times they were baffled and greeted his revelation with a tremendous groan. There appeared to be no definite routine and townspeople, policemen, Indians and this one gringo had a wonderful time placing grains of corn onto colored pictures. Cost of each game was a five *centavo* coin (2¢ U.S.) and the prize was half of the fees collected. On the second game I was lucky enough to win a handful of coins. With this loot I played for another hour and was congratulated on my luck at least two-dozen times.

Near the bingo game, parish mothers were operating a grab-bag concession where players selected a bit of paper from a drum and were given the prize listed. Most prizes were printed cutouts, dolls, books or tin toys. Hanging high in the booth were tiny dolls and a toy sewing machine all the children eyed hungrily.

Fresh meat was sold in street markets by the piece. The impressive shopper's basket is filled with other purchases.

Off to one side, for men only, there was a chuck-a-luck game. An ice cream concession served excellent cream with soft drinks available next door. The lunch stand cooked meals to order on a charcoal fire and served steak, beans and rice. Plus cups of very strong coffee.

Fr. Antonio displayed delightful warmth while I was taking motion pictures of *turno* action. A handful of town rowdies purposely stood in the way and wouldn't move. When I told the padre about my problem he gave them the devil in a good grade of barroom Spanish. As the gang ran away down the street under onslaught of the padre's comments he picked up a fist-size rock and threw it just far enough to miss the last straggler. A few minutes later I saw him giving each urchin a five *centavo* coin for ice cream.

Every half hour, perhaps to remind the festive throng of their duty to spend money, bells of the church were rung for a full minute. The bell-ringer climbed a ladder to access the 20-foot-high temporary platform from which he swung short clapper ropes to begin the ear-splitting serenade. *Turno* activity stopped dead from inability to hear oneself think rather than from any amount of religious fervor. My subsequent departure was somewhat emotional as many parish members came over to say goodbye and wish me good luck and Godspeed for the rest of my journey to Panama.

A day or so later I visited the small coastal village of La Herradura. Friends had told me it was a lovely place where sea water nearly surrounded the village site on marshland jutting into a shallow bay. The beachward road was graveled dirt all the way and more or less free from ruts until I faced troublesome deep patches of sand leading into the village. A fair was in progress and the unpaved village street was alive with people, policemen and drunks.

Motoring slowly through the crowd was made even more difficult by horsemen eager to race the little motorcycle. Nothing doing. The police had enough trouble without my trying their patience further. After I parked a posse of drunken riders thundered past, scattered random children right and left and pulled their horses up by the merry-go-round. They threw money at the ticket vendor, pushed the operator to one side and jumped aboard the spinning platform so each could mount a wooden horse of their choosing. Kids couldn't have had more fun than these grown men whooping and hollering as they spun around and around. But circular motion was too much for their stomachs as first one then another became violently ill and heaved all over the place. Policemen finally arrived in force and stopped the machinery. Both sick and well were hauled off their silent steeds and sternly warned to ride their own horses and leave the kid stuff alone. By this time most seemed so sick they couldn't really care and may have been relieved that someone had stopped their foolishness.

His living was made, and family fed, by rowing to one of the many islands, cutting wood and bringing it back for sale in the village.

A half-block away I rode off the village street and entered a narrow foot path toward the beach. Families on their way to town were astonished to see a bike plowing along their sand pathway but stepped aside to give me room while shouting a cheery greeting as I chugged by. At the beach-front cantina I ordered a beer and the proprietor, an elderly woman, sat with me to find out what I was doing so far from home. I explained about the trip and she interpreted my story in more understandable Spanish for the other patrons. While she talked there was time to appreciate my surroundings of crudely made tables and chairs scattered over a recently broomed dirt floor. The counter and ice box were under an extended shed roof hung on the side of a one-room house where I imagined that the family lived. A juke box in one corner of the cantina was protected by barbed wire and wood fencing. The owner told me that occasionally drunks became unhappy with the music and would try to kick the machine into submissive silence. While she was talking I could feel pressure on my feet under the table. This was too much. There was no objection to telling about my trip but she was not really my type.

A minute or two later she left and the rhythmic pressures continued until my dive under the table destroyed the mysterious romance. One of several pigs that were circulating to keep the floor clean had discovered my boots and was industriously licking at the old tallow waterproofing. When my hostess returned there was a definite change in her attitude. She confidentially whispered that I must leave the village before nightfall.

She repeated the warning several times to be certain I understood her urgency and as the sun was nearing the horizon I left for the bay shore. The tripod and camera were placed in a desirable site and I waited for the usual colorful rays of sunset. Children playing in the vicinity had disappeared behind nearby buildings to watch my actions. As soon as it was evident they were not to be photographed they resumed play and paid little attention to me. I watched them for a while then returned to my tripod. What a surprise. In only a few minutes the tide had come in and what had been dry land was now under water. I splashed out to the equipment and moved it to a high spot. The sun set without clouds or sky colors about the time a native boatman paddled toward land with a load of wood. With his permission I shot color film while he unloaded. He had not asked for money but I decided to pay for the pictures and asked which children were his. He pointed to the two youngest unclothed boys and shouted "*Gracias!*" as I gave each one a 25 *centavo* coin. By this time the water had edged near the bike, which spurred a hurried departure through the noisy village street before night fell.

Because my stay in El Salvador had to be extended to complete research for magazine stories, I experienced a gentle means of raising money for government services: *papel oficial* or official paper. Handsomely engraved, bonded and stamped, it was the only paper on which petitioners could solicit assistance from a government office. To obtain permission to keep the bike in the county for another month I bought a sheet for 30 *centavos*, asked the *aduana* secretary to type my request in Spanish, watched an officer read everything twice then thanked him for initialing it. Five copies were typed on plain paper and one was given to me.

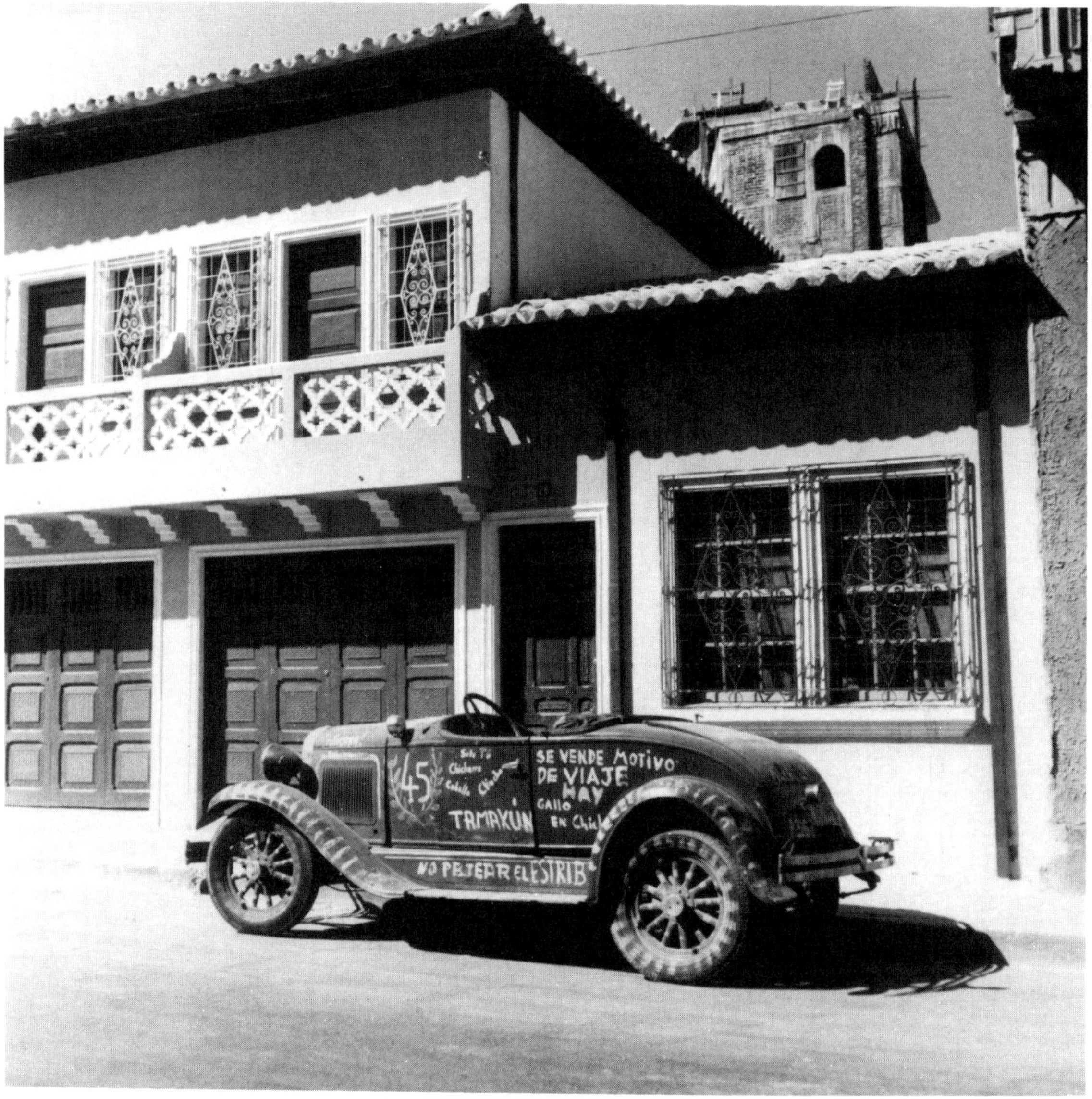

There was nothing bashful about the owner of this roadster in making sure that everyone knew his car was for sale.

An extension from the *migracion* office was easier. A friend employed in another government area whispered a few words to the guard, we bypassed a long line of waiting tourists, entered the director's suite, were introduced and sipped coffee while discussing business. After social graces were cared for the chief of El Salvador's immigration service agreed that I could remain as long as I wished and wrote permission to do so onto my temporary residence permit.

Somewhere during this busy day I heard a Spanish proverb that translates as "For every person who gets up early in the morning there is someone who does not sleep that night." Which seems to have predicted my again seeing the Mexican "air force captain" I met at the Talisman border station in Tapachula. As I was walking up Calle Arce that afternoon I saw the Mexican hot-airman driving a new Mercury. This was such a surprise that later I mentioned it to a friend who was linked to the police department. My information did not surprise him. He told me that El Salvador knew about the four-flusher, had agents following him and were only waiting for the most productive moment to pick him up for interrogation.

One Sunday a friend invited me to visit *Hacienda Nueva* a large *finca* (ranch) on the outskirts of San Salvador. In an area of ten by thirty miles, coffee, cattle, corn, beans and rice were produced under the supervision of an ex-army officer from neighboring Honduras. At home he had once been active in politics until a revolution forced hurried departure to the comparative safety of El Salvador where he carried a nickel-plated Colt for protection. The former colonel took great pride in telling me about the ranch, its fine purebred cattle, large fruit orchard, good-looking horses and the owner's magnificent house. What a dream. It was a huge ground-level building with five bedrooms, an enormous living/dining room combination, primitive bathroom facilities and three full-time servants to care for guests.

In one block of San Salvador there were three fine motorcycles including this unusual Horex with deep engine fins.

This hard-tail Zundapp had an engine resembling that in the BMW of the same period, pictured below.

The beautiful BMW R-51/2 had only arrived in San Salvador a few weeks before I found it at the curb.

Behind the funeral car and walking mourners there was a procession of flower-decorated passenger cars containing members of the family.

Fresh coconuts are easily opened,
by someone else, with a very sharp machete
and an extremely steady hand.

Several of the younger farm employees introduced me to really fresh coconuts. They led me from tree to tree, pointed to different sizes and qualities of nuts and finally gave a full-dress demonstration of obtaining coconut milk. The longest ladder on the *finca* was propped against a tree so a youth of 10 or 12 could romp up the rungs and bombard us with ripe nuts. Each of us carried one as we retreated to the ranch-house porch. They were opened by a farm-hand who braced a nut in his bare hand while hacking at the top with a razor-sharp machete. After the first nut was open, as a guest I had to sample the warm watery liquid which was nearly clear and tasted nothing at all like coconut. From then on we used fresh coconut milk as a dandy chaser for the Colonel's excellent local brandy.

Near noon or several drinks later, whichever came first, I was asked what I would like for lunch. Casually I pointed in the general direction of a nearby chicken. A lad caught the unsuspecting fowl, macheted the head and carried the bleeding handful to the kitchen quicker than it takes to read this. Soon afterward one chicken and Carroll were face to face at the lunch table with the chicken being a tasty loser. The last bits of food were quickly polished off when the colonel decided to demonstrate his shooting ability with a 22-caliber rifle from the dining room wall. Ranch hands, their boss and we guests trooped back to the porch. A small hole was excavated to accept a five *centavo* coin in the trunk of a tree about 50 feet away. The colonel's two shots were so blurred by brandy they didn't come close to the tree let alone hit the coin. Next to shoot was Humberto who had brought me to the ranch. His first shot knocked the coin from the tree. The second caused a bit of bark to fly into the air.

Then it was my turn.

The rifle was a model I had used before and this asset, plus a barrel of luck, helped my first slug send the coin spinning off into the dusty driveway. It was replaced amid dead silence. My last shot just had to be as good. I raised the rifle, took careful aim, held my breath and squeezed the trigger exactly as the book says. "Crack!" and the coin disappeared. Discretion being the better part of valor I handed the rifle to the Colonel, said "This is a very good gun," and declined to do more shooting.

Our host then announced that we should go horseback riding, a sport at which I am enormously unskilled. Three beasts were brought from the stable and tied to the porch. Ranch hands did the saddling then stood back to watch.

The colonel and my friend Humberto mounted flawlessley and calmly watched while I tried to scramble aboard. First a foot in the left stirrup, grasp the handle on the saddle and pull. I pulled and didn't rise an inch. The belly-band was so loose the saddle rolled over and hung below like a leather jock strap, which looked even sillier on the mare. Someone resaddled the poor animal and goosed me aboard. It was a very fine fast ride with every moment thought to be my last until we slowed through heavy underbrush, which permitted my taking a few very cautious glances at passing scenery.

On our way back to the stables a sudden spurt of horsey energy broke a rein. This was reason enough for said horse to enjoy a full gallop which fortunately stopped, before I bounced off, at a fence too high for jumping. The reins were repaired with Boy Scout knots, then a stirrup broke. The colonel fixed it but the leather tore again and I rode the last mile with one leg flapping in the breeze. After we dismounted our host was thoughtful enough to direct me to a hammock for an overdue *siesta*. This was not to last long. The hammock allowed about three swings before it dropped me onto a very hard concrete tiled floor. In short, the colonel had gotten even for my accidental sharpshooting.

Enough is enough and I asked to be excused. My friend, Humberto, was collected from his nap in a chair and we were given two coconuts to hang on the bike's tail-light bracket. The late tropical afternoon was splendid for riding and we thumped along happily until two traffic policemen stopped us at an intersection for a routine inspection. During the conversation my fender-riding partner confidentially wondered if we could beat the old police Harleys. "Of course we can," I replied with more confidence than wisdom.

All the shorter policeman wanted to know was how did I expect the tiny BSA to be faster than his big Harley.

For about 75 cents a day (U.S.) these men shoveled river sand for use in San Salvador construction projects.

The challenge was made and one officer asked, "How do you expect your little one-cylinder machine to keep up with my big *moto*?"

"We'll show you," Humberto replied and the race was on.

The first three-abreast start was a dud because one of the policeman lost his cap and we stopped while he retrieved the sign of authority. On the second start I was able to get the jump on both officers and for the next 12 miles it was a mad scramble along a now-dark, twisting canyon road littered with slippery ox dumpings. Luckily the BSA could gear down for the curves and then scream onto the straight-away like a wheeled rocket. The policemen made up a little lost time on the same straights but we were able to gain considerable distance by out-cornering them. Finally the next town came into view past an *Alto* sign for the city limits' traffic control station of Santa Ana.

I parked and we flopped on the grass to pretend a non-existent nonchalance. A full minute later two bobbing headlights appeared and the Harleys slid to a stop. Both policemen insisted we had just arrived in their shouted questions to the control station guard. He grinned and swore by all the patron saints that we had been resting on the grass for at least three or four minutes. Both motor officers accepted invitations to ride the BSA's rear fender. This would have been fun but the first man nearly broke my ribs with excitement when the front wheel became light as we accelerated. The second man was a bit more cool about such antics. We continued three-abreast into San Salvador as a small parade of two police motorcycles and a BSA single. In front of the national palace the patrolmen turned off to their barracks while Humberto and I headed for cold beer.

Several days later I was at the national police headquarters obtaining magazine article information about motorcycle registrations (396 in 1950) and requesting a Salvador license plate for the BSA. While visiting with the chief of transit police I learned that his patrolmen had told him of the speedy little single. He asked a goodly number of sharp questions about motorcycles before giving me the punch line, "Would you like to race me?" I declined with thanks as earlier he had previously mentioned riding a brand new more powerful Police Special.

One Sunday I decided to visit the village of Izalco at the base of the nation's famous volcano known as the "Lighthouse of Central America." Eruptions were at one time so constant that ocean-going vessels used the volcano's glow and smoke against the sky as an aid to navigation. By 1950 the crater was spouting infrequently and I was told that the best way

There was little done to fight this furniture store fire because block walls of the building protected adjoining property.

to take a picture would be to wait. A walk through the village disclosed the second floor above the community store as the ideal site for picture taking. The owner was agreeable and led me upstairs to a bedroom balcony. He left, I raised the tripod, attached the loaded camera and waited for action. It was not long in coming.

While making these preparations I had not noticed that a most attractive woman of 17 or 18 years was also in the room. She was slender except where she should have been plump, was very friendly and interested in everything. Where did I come from? How did the camera work? On a motorcycle? Plus requesting a dozen other odds and ends of information. Then she decided to investigate the contents of my camera case, which was next to the bed. Her interest was inspiring until all hell broke loose. From the corner of my eye I caught the volcano begin to erupt at the same time I heard the stairs creak and the store owner call out for his daughter (wife?). I went for the camera but was so confused I exposed three pictures on the same sheet of Kodachrome before reloading to shoot one that turned out to be usable. Meanwhile the man must have discovered worry because he remained in the bedroom until the last picture had been taken, before leading all of us downstairs.

That evening I was sleeping the sleep of a frustrated man. Dreaming involved the store owner being very unhappy and reaching for his shotgun. While he was fumbling a shell into the chamber I kissed his woman good-by, leaped on my trusty iron and accelerated out of Izalco with the sound of shots ringing in my ears. The explosions seemed so real I could hear the bullets whiz past. Then it dawned on my sleep-fogged brain; there were genuine gun shots outside the pension. I heard people running down the street, calling to one another, then more shots. In minutes I too was on the street and thinking fast to understand the excited conversations I could overhear. A nearby furniture store was on fire and policemen had sounded the alarm by firing their handguns into the air.

The building was burning rapidly with flames 50 feet high. Families next door had moved their belongings into the street by the time the fire department arrived. In their hurry the hydrant connection was poorly made. When the water was turned on the hose blew off and nearby onlookers were doused. The hydrant was shut down, the hose ring properly tightened and water turned on again. This time the firemen neglected to hold down the nozzle end of the hose and it whipped back and forth to spray policemen and more of the innocent bystanders.

Firemen finally subdued the wandering nozzle about the time an electrical crew disconnected power to the burning store and rigged floodlights on an opposite building. Eventually a truck with emergency police arrived and they lined up in a military formation. German army

The Rio Lempa river was to be dammed at this point for installation of a major hydro-electric plant to ease El Salvador's power shortage.

officers must have trained the police because after orders were issued, several of the sleepy men began goose-stepping before remembering to march like their fellow officers. An hour after I awoke the fire was out and only a few police remained in the street to guard the meager belongings of the evacuated families.

While researching an article about the Rio Lempa hydro-electric project I passed through the village of Ilobasco. In the central square next to the fountain about 50 earthenware pots and tins were lined up like eager theatre goers. Each one carried a chalked number. While I was poking around the village a policeman inquired about my interest in the pots. I asked him why numbers on pots. He explained that electric power was so limited that the Ilobasco water pump could only be turned on for two hours each day. A system of water rationing had been worked out with village women who obtained water from the fountain. As he found time the

Two members of the staff at
El Salvador's National Tourist Office
sent me off to Honduras with their best wishes.

policeman marked their pots beginning with No. 1 closest to the fountain. By 6:30 P.M., when the water was turned on, women were waiting in the square with their pot number saving a position in line. On the basis of one container to the household, we estimated there were only about 200 gallons of water per day for Ilobasco.

My last days in El Salvador were days of unusual activity. The national police had rounded up known trouble makers, civil rights were suspended and Carroll needed visas and vehicle export paperwork to leave. Because of such internal unrest it took the best portion of a full day to clear the involved government offices. Early the final morning I went to the *turismo* office for last-minute mail and farewells to the staff, which had been so helpful.

It wasn't much of an event as the sister of one of the secretaries was seriously ill in the city hospital. All I could do was offer sympathy and plan to leave quietly. While shaking hands with the secretary I mentioned having the type of blood that can be given to almost anyone. A half hour later at the pension, while checking out, I received a telephone call. "Would you give the ill woman a transfusion? If you would, the doctor could operate and perhaps save her life." I considered it not to be a problem and within a few minutes the *turismo* station wagon arrived. On the way to the hospital I was briefed on the sister's trouble. She had experienced internal bleeding but did not like her doctor so did nothing. Soon it was too late for medication and an operation was the next step.

At the Cuscatlan toll bridge, on the
way to Honduras, the girl in the white dress tried
to sell me her watermelon. "In yo' lap," she said.

The four must have done a good job of repairing my punctured tube because it carried El Salvador air all the way to Panama.

But she was weak from loss of blood and there was not enough money in the family to pay for a transfusion. At the hospital the procedure of typing and taking blood was, as usual, painless and quick. However my friends of the *turismo* staff clustered around the head of the bed and complained about how sick they had become from watching my blood spurt into the hanging bottle. When finished I was introduced to the husband of the woman for whom they had bled me. He expressed amazement that a stranger would give blood for his wife and blessed his thanks with tears. On the way back to the pension the woman's sister wanted every detail of giving blood as she had not watched. I explained the procedure then, after moments of embarrassed silence, she asked, "What did the family give you as payment for the blood? Did you know it would have cost them ₡90 ($36 U.S.) if you had had not given it?"

I replied that "thanks" was enough. She said something about it being all right for a friend but I didn't even know the woman. Then she added, under her breath in Spanish, "The gringo is crazy." At the pension I said farewell.

Still a little weak from lost liquid I took a 45-minute nap then paid for lodgings, loaded the bike (6170 miles) and headed out on the paved highway to San Miguel near the border with Honduras. It should have been a pleasant ride through the gentle mountain scenery but I was all over the road and made several stops to rest. When the main street of San Miguel hove into view (6255 miles) I found the biggest hotel, 23 rooms, and flopped until the waiter woke me to eat before they closed the dining room.

My exit from El Salvador was highly informal
at a border control station far less impressive than
that at the more heavily traveled frontier with Guatemala.

Warnings had been frequent about the poor roads in Honduras so I made an early start about 6:30 that morning and within ten miles had left the pavement for dusty graded dirt and my first flat tire; in the village of Santa Rosa de Lima. Nails were so expensive in Latin America that I'm certain it was the only brand new loose nail in the entire nation. Or was it tossed by the repair shop located just 150 feet behind the flat? An hour and four assistants later the tube was repaired, luggage replaced, cola enjoyed and the departure from El Salvador resumed.

A few miles farther and I was at the frontier, 130 miles from San Salvador. A five-minute "check out" and a ₡1 (40¢ U.S.) tax stamp was all the permission needed to cross the line and begin over 100 miles of boondocking to the capital of Honduras.

Delegacion de Migracion...Amatillo
Sala Para Hond...Fecha: 13-3-51

Militar...El Amatillo...Honduras
Para Tegucigalpa...13-3-51

The Honduras frontier control point was large and messy with guards in civilian clothes wearing military insignia as their sign of authority. Without charge my passport was stamped and the luggage given a cursory examination. From El Amatillo *La Carretera Interamericana* was very good dirt to a police inspection and traffic control station at Jicaro Galán. This was the intersection with the sideroad to Tegucigalpa, the capital city of Honduras, that had been the subject of dire warnings from my friends in El Salvador. Officers at the junction logged my name, BSA documentation and license number. At the same time I arrived, a truck-load of water pipe pulled out. After the police routine it took only a few minutes to catch the truck and ask the driver to carry my luggage. He was agreeable and I dumped everything I could spare on top of the pipe, with delivery in Tegucigalpa promised for the following day about noon.

The next 75 miles of roadway, the only vehicle entry into Tegucigalpa, proved to be a five-hour first-and second-gear grind all the way. It was dusty and rough with iguanas scurrying across the road at frequent intervals to keep drivers and riders alert. Much of the route was not only used by motor vehicles but also for the run-off of rainstorms that had massaged the surface into an overused streambed of gullies and random rocks. There were few farms and only one small village, where I stopped for a cold drink. My average speed of about 15 miles an hour had the bike's front and rear suspension frequently bottoming and topping. But there was no way I was going to hurry and risk breaking machinery, with spare parts not likely to be found in the next bamboo hut. A few days later I learned that trucks with passengers take 12 hours for the trip, trucks with large loads (such as pipe) take 18 to 24 hours and the "highway" was better than ever. After I reached the capital's airport, the four miles of Honduras' only rural pavement was easy riding to the city.

One of the better sections of the "highway" into Tegucigalpa and its impossible-to-miss-a-rock surface.

The BSA was cleaned and polished for its picture with us (Carroll, Stradling and Liebers; L to R) in front of Liebers' Tegucigalpa warehouse.

It was surprising the number of pedestrians who stopped to read about the BSA's travels and discuss its arrival from California.

Tegucigalpa (6471 miles) was found to be a lovely place with clean narrow streets, most of which were one-way without stop signs. A corner policeman wearing a tropical pith helmet was no help with directions but a pedestrian told me that the recommended pension was, "Up the street one block."

The next day at the office of the local BSA dealer I met H. C. Stradling, of B.S.A. Cycles, Birmingham, England. As their overseas representative, Stradling happened to have arrived in Honduras the same day I bounced in. His Honduras dealer, Max Liebers, a Swiss, had complained that he could not get an adequate stock and had over 30 motorcycles on back order. Stradling explained that materials for BSA production were on allocation from the (British) Board of Trade and the company was building at the rate of 1500 units a week, 75 percent of which were exported. Liebers told me there were 131 motorcycles in Honduras in 1951 of which 35 were BSAs. My B-33 single would sell for Ł (*lempira*) 1250. ($625 U.S.) which was about a year's income for a clerical worker. Stradling left the following morning for Nicaragua and I remained in Tegucigalpa for additional days of sightseeing. While I was there Liebers donated a Honduras license plate for my collection, arranged a newspaper interview and planted the BSA in his show-window with a poster explaining its arrival from California.

At the Boarding House Americana a young woman, who said she worked for a Mexican airline, sat with me in the pension dining room and worked at adding words to my Spanish vocabulary. One day when I arrived in time for lunch she was feeding a friend's month-old baby. My not-too-wise salutation was "*Muey rapido*" (Fast work), which every ear in the room must have heard too clearly.

The corner policeman was no help in finding my lodgings which were a block away. As in many nations of Central America, the street direction signs also pitched soft drinks.

All forms of transportation were in use in downtown Tegucigalpa, which was the smallest of Central America's capital cities.

In a lovely park overlooking the city I found this collection of Mayan figures which appeared to be replicas rather than originals.

In front of the national palace I asked for directions to the roadway leaving Honduras toward Nicaragua.

There was a wave of repetition in several languages amid noisy laughter of other guests matched by the big grin on my table-mate's face. Later she decided I was lonely and introduced me to 14 female middle-school basketball players from Guatemala who had arrived to play the local champions. The girls asked many questions, one of which was, "How many children do you have?" I very carefully explained that I could not be certain, as none of the seven wives allowed by my (mythical) religion had written for three weeks. From then on I only had to come near to cause their conversation to buzz about an American with seven wives.

The manager of the Tela Railroad office, which represented the banana company and freight services, telephoned one morning to tell me that I had a package in customs. It was additional film for which I paid Ł 3 ($1.50 U.S.) as the import fee. The rest of the morning was used to write letters and visit with Liebers. He and his manager took the bike for a ride. They returned enthusiastic about its performance and comfort of the new plunger-type spring frame.

American coins circulated freely in Honduras because the *lempira*, which exchanged at 50¢ U.S., was almost exactly the same size as our half-dollar. The movie house on the central plaza was a government monopoly which charged 30 *centavos* (15¢ U.S.) for a show in an impressive house where the best seats were on the sides of the walls as in a legitimate theatre. Outside I noticed that the city's fire hydrants were in chambers below the

The military traffic control post and customs office at Jicaro Galan was in this building which included a siesta hammock just inside the door.

A bit of cargo fell off the bike as this passenger truck approached and the man on the roof threw me a length of rope with a "Good Luck" as he waved goodbye.

Someone washed the bike while I overnighted in this tiny Honduras hotel. The manager, his girl-friend and the cook were on hand when I left for Nicaragua.

sidewalks and could be accessed only by lifting a heavy lid. Because the pension was nearby, there was no way to ignore noisy public-address speakers around the plaza that continually blared announcements and music from the government radio station. Near the edge of town raising and lowering the national flag was accompanied by a military band concert in front of the *Palacio Nacional.*

Leaving Honduras was more involved than coming in. I had to get my passport visa extended to enter Nicaragua, then inspected and stamped three times: by the *Ministerio de Relaciones Exterior* (foreign office), *Ministerio de Guerro, Marina y Aviacion* (war department) and by the *Departmento de Investigations, Policia Nacional* (police department). To lighten my load I air-shipped excess baggage to San Jose, Costa Rica. The bike was gassed the next morning for Ł 1 (50¢ U.S.) a gallon, we were photographed in front of the *Palacio Nacional* and I was off to again ride that miserable 75 miles of national riverbed. The moment I passed Tegucigalpa's airport and left the nation's four miles of paved highway it was slow-going all over again. Five hours later, at Jicaro Galan, I rejoined *La Carretera Interamericana* and its relatively smooth dirt to my overnight in a small hotel in San Marcos de Colon, a few miles from the frontier.

Early the next morning I presented myself to the Honduran border guards and was logged through into Nicaragua.

Salio 20 de Marzo 1951
Administracion de Aduana
El Espina...Choluteca, Honduras

There must have been little for the staff of this Honduras aduana to do as the road appeared to have been seldom used past this point.

I was carefully logged out of Honduras and the passport stamped at this dining table under the aduana porch.

Cuartel General de Civil Batallon
Guardin Nacional de Nicaragua...20 Marzo

Inspection and signing a handful of forms at the Nicaraguan border shack were completed in a few minutes and we departed through rolling hills along a graded one-car-wide dirt road which was *La Carretera Interamericana* in Nicaragua. Eight miles of this brought me to the army garrison village of Somoto. On the outskirts there was a modern overhead electric traffic signal above the dirt which was controlled from a roadside guard-house. Apparently we appeared harmless as the green light glowed to permit uninterrupted entry. More inspections in offices two blocks apart were no problem but the gasoline news was all bad.

The tank truck that usually serviced Somoto had not been seen for a week. Neither of the village's two pumps had fuel and most local vehicles were stalled. A careful look into my tank wasn't reassuring but I decided to ride on, hoping to make it to the next fuel stop 75 miles further. My estimate was really poor and in a deserted section of nowhere the thumper stopped thumping. Its reserve was good for about 15 miles, which was little help when compared to a map that displayed nothing for the next 40 miles. There was no reason to bake in the tropic sun so I restarted but stopped in nearly the same instant as a lumber truck appeared around the bend ahead. I hailed the driver, explained my problem and was deeply grateful when he produced a five-gallon can of gas to fill my three-gallon tank. I tried my best to pay him but he would have none of it and took additional time give me details of road conditions ahead.

There was no need to open the gate because the bike passed easily through the opening used for foot traffic between Nicaragua and Honduras.

While motoring into Managua I too passed under the decorated arches carried by this religious group with the unusually tall float.

Traffic on downtown streets was often blocked by religious processions led by women wearing black shawls.

It took hard work to be an entrepreneur in Managua as demonstrated by the homemade front wheels on this parcel delivery cart.

My subsequent arrival in Nicaragua's capital, Managua, was uneventful except for riding the wrong way on a one-way street and stopping only inches from a huge gasoline truck. The city was in the midst of holy days celebrations which complicated my search for housing as most hotels were full. Eventually a suitable room was found for ₡ 15 (*cordobas*) ($2.25 U.S.) which included meals. For safekeeping I rode the BSA over the sidewalk, up a few steps, through the lobby and parked it in the patio.

Religious holidays in Nicaragua were days of ceremony and the locals did not approve of motor vehicle use during their holy days. Water and rocks were thrown at me, and elderly ladies snapped their shawls in my direction, when I attempted to tour Managua on Sunday. There were many processions that involved church groups parading their patron saint's statue behind the music of a marching band. A few nighttime marches included portable gasoline generators to illuminate the multiple colored lights carried by children. Among sidewalk watchers the young men and women threw confetti at each other and made arrangements to meet later for more energetic socializing.

Another portion of my Latin American education was completed in Nicaragua. Along the route there had been many signs which advertised "Mejoral" in bright colors. Because they were often adjacent to cola advertising I assumed that "Mejoral" was another Latin refreshment and intended to sample it with my next meal in a restaurant. Fortunately knowledge came before disaster. It seemed that although "Mejoral" was advertised to cure headaches it was better known as a potent laxative.

Perhaps I did not remain in Managua long enough to appreciate its values, as my daily journal reflects rather unfortunate opinions of the relatively impoverished community. "One fire station for entire city...a push cart knocks over a bicyclist and the boys argue...baskets on carriers' heads, one wears a live squirrel for decoration...two little girls in a doorway picking lice from each other's hair...the old man, proud and rigidly upright, whipping a tired horse up the street...a street cleaning machine that can only fill its water tank at the fire station...men, boys and sturdy women pushing wooden-wheeled carts...a case of empty cola bottles passes by on the head of a carrier who returns in minutes with a case of full bottles...the dignified family of well-dressed Indians walking in the center of the street carrying bundles on their heads...public transportation made from retired school busses with the top cut down to window sill level...a boy running his push cart down hill and laboring back up with a load...two kids on bikes miss the corner and crash head-over-heels against a curb...a youth kisses his girl then glances to see if I had noticed...the blind beggar of about ten, with his five-year-old companion who cried on command...logs and rocks laid across main highways to prevent car movement during holy days...being told that if you know

In the small town of Rivas the religious procession included almost the entire population with some of the younger women being dressed in white.

the right people you can make money, if not, forget it...street money changers offering various rates on *cordobas* (₡) for dollars....the luncheon companion who much too loudly warned me to be aware of government spies."

Permission to leave Nicaragua was arranged with short visits to two government offices where clerks shook their heads sadly when told I was traveling to Costa Rica on a motorcycle. Consensus was: First, I must be crazy. Second, I would never get there. Third, the road to Costa Rica did not exist. However conversations with private citizens had given hope of riding all the way although the route was reputed to be in fearful condition.

Following suggestions I rode only to the border town of Rivas (6869 miles) to spend the night. After checking in at the Hotel Central, where the bed was a canvas cot without sheets or blankets, I gassed the BSA and rode around Rivas on its totally unpaved streets. At one point I passed a convent behind the sheet-iron church and stopped to listen as eight nuns prayed in unison. Their soothing voices were an impressive prelude to a late-afternoon holy days parade in which it seemed that everyone in Rivas followed their saint's statue through city streets.

After the parade I decided to visit the hotel's toilet. None was to be found so I asked the waiter where the *tocador* was. He shrugged his shoulders so I asked for the "toilet" in hopes he knew an English word. More shrugs. I tried *bano* (Bath). He grinned and shook his head again. *excusar* (excuse) didn't work. I asked for the *agua caja* (water box) and he brought me a glass of water. I showed him toilet paper I carried and he produced a new roll. I thought I told him "I want to make water" and he showed me the hotel's well.

This was great for the one night in Rivas
except for the low partition on the right
which failed to inhibit a romantic commotion next door.

Moments after this picture was taken I discovered that the gas tank had fractured and was leaking. A fat chunk of what appeared to be tree gum was used for the repair.

Finally the lad decided there was one thing I had not asked for and pointed to an outhouse, of mahogany planks no less, parked over a hole in the ground. Then he explained that in Rivas, it is the *escusado e inodora*, which somewhat translates into "a place to be excused while indoors," so he said. At the same time I discovered that the privy was a measured 20 feet from the well from which the hotel's washing, cooking and drinking water was taken. Reason enough I drank only beer with dinner while ignoring pigs and chickens circulating in the dining patio for scraps of food.

Sunday morning found me up early for a fresh start toward another "worst stretch" of *La Carretera Interamericana*. After checking out from the hotel for ₡13.50 ($2.00 U.S.), which included a noisy discussion over the amount of change returned by the owner, I loaded the bike, which had been parked in a carpenter's yard behind the hotel. As I tilted the machine to mount I noticed liquid dribble over the gas tank and found that the tank had fractured where it attached to the steering throat. Such an unpleasant surprise wasn't needed. The carpenter was nearby and I asked if there were any mechanic's shops open. "Holy days," he replied and shook his head. We reinspected the fracture and he came up with a solution. From the workshop he produced a lump of what seemed to be tree gum, which was unaffected when I smeared gasoline on it. We wiped the tank dry with newspaper and I pressed a thick layer of gum over and around the crack. It didn't leak when the machine was upright so I left.

At the edge of Rivas I had to weave around road obstructions and accept taunts from church-going women who objected to my riding during holy days. From there to the border was 20 miles on a wide graveled road of stateside quality, perhaps for no better reason than once it had been completed there was little reason for anyone to drive to the border from which one should go no further. I stopped along the way to take several pictures, one of which was of the warning sign on a wooden bridge by Lake Nicaragua. The sign stated that ten tons was the load limit for timbers that swayed uncomfortably under a bike, its luggage and Carroll.

At the Nicaragua/Costa Rica frontier I almost ran over an armed guard pacing back and forth across the roadway in front of a gated fence. To miss him I swerved into the first barnlike building, which turned out to be his barracks. The next building was for travelers and, amazingly enough, was processing a party of Costa Ricans on their way home. They had driven to Nicaragua to spend holy days with friends in Managua. Both men spoke English and while papers were being stamped I answered questions about motorcycles. Realizing that I might have trouble on the road ahead they offered to wait for me at a distant rest point. If I did not show up for an hour or so they said they would backtrack to find me.

Then it was my turn. My passport and personal entry documents were satisfactory but "Where is the entry permit for the motorcycle?" the guard asked. I explained that he had everything given to me in Somoto and what else was I supposed to have. The man described a sheet allowing the cycle to enter Nicaragua on which a small tax would have been paid. Worry must have shown all over my face as he appeared a little sad at being the bearer of such bad tidings. Then it struck. I had paid the tax and words tumbled all over each other in my eagerness to explain. In Somoto, the *aduanero* had placed a stamp at both top and bottom of a paper but had kept the whole works. My description of the application of stamps must have been graphic because another officer asked for a repeat performance. With Shakespearean gestures I went through the act again. (One can be very convincing when failure means riding 500 miles back for a piece of paper, then return 500 miles to where you were in the first place.) My second explanation was enough. A bit of very rapid Spanish flew between the two men, they stamped my papers and pointed me toward the gate now open into Costa Rica.

Guardia Nacional de Nicaragua
Peña Blanca...25/3...Salida

Republica de Costa Rica...La Cruz
Admitido...Fecha: 25/3/51

The open gate into Costa Rica made an easy passage to its combined *aduana* and guard barracks, which was a rambling two-storey building with laundry hanging from its back balcony rails. No formality here. The officers wore jeans and cowboy boots and packed their side-arm in a holster on the leg. They came to where I parked and verified my name, address and destination. While I replaced my passport into its waterproof packet the Costa Rican party pulled out and disappeared. A guard pointed in the same general direction, which was a plowed field with ruts that led through a small gully, under a large tree and across a bumpy meadow past two bored cows. About 300 yards farther the road split and I turned onto the more-traveled right fork. It was a smooth ride until a down slope brought me face to face with a river about 150 feet wide.

I had been warned to expect trouble but this was much too soon. After parking the bike on the river bank, I splashed around trying to find the ford. It appeared that every driver had used his own idea of the best crossing which turned my choices into "Nothing ventured nothing gained." Cameras were left on the bank and I straddled the bike for a wet ride. It was. After bumping and splashing for about 15 feet of stoned river bottom the front wheel hit an unseen obstacle and I was stuck. "Damn" was only one of many fine words applicd to a completely unresisting motorcycle. Water ran over the top of my boots as I sweated the front wheel free but forward motion was only a good idea because the rear tire now spun in watery sand.

The frontier monument between Nicaragua, to the left, is only is only a few feet from the Costa Rica customs house and barracks on the right.

The Costa Rican party had almost completed border-crossing formalities by the time I reached their nation's frontier post.

Over the gurgle of the bike's underwater exhaust I heard automobile engines laboring in gear as two ancient jeeps appeared on the opposite bank. One of the drivers shouted a question about my destination. To my response, he called back in good English, "San Jose! This road doesn't go to San Jose. You should take the other road." He obviously meant the left fork, which appeared as though it had not been used for two decades. They dismounted and splashed over to the bike to help me carry the dripping beast to dry land. One man suggested that a ride back to California might be easier than the next 200 miles to San Jose. After wishing me good luck they left me alone to contemplate the virtues of an engine that starts easily. Two kicks and there was life demonstrated by gallons of river water spraying from the exhaust outlet. I rode back to the fork and turned right onto the proper route through equally desolate territory.

Not only was the cool water almost up to my knees
but the bottom of the river was just as
lumpy as the near shore.

A subsequent situation was the needful
draining of water from my riding boots.
(As you've guessed, my camera had a self-timer.)

For many miles the Interamerican Highway included random crossings made of cut logs laid in a ravine to allow vehicle passage.

In other sections the streams had to be ridden through to continue along the one-lane "highway" in its tunnel of tropic underbrush and trees.

This pair of ruts wandered around rocks of virgin severity for a nearly a mile before passing through a grove of trees, down another steep slope to a narrow stream with a rocky bottom. Vehicles had pressed the ford somewhat level and this time passage was easy. On the opposite side a most interesting collection of river-bank oil spots indicated that a vehicle or two had crashed its crankcase and made the passage at the cost of the engine's life-blood. It took two starts to climb the steep 30-foot stream bank, only to find that the same stream had doubled back. The crossing performance was: unload camera bags, cross the stream on foot to find the best passage, return, ride over, wade back for cameras, return to motorcycle, drain boots, remount, kick and ride off.

The narrow twisting road was a jeep's nightmare. It squeezed through dense overhanging brush, which made a tunnel of the tropical jungle, with a few climbs so steep the bike had to be peg-ridden with weight forward to keep the front wheel on the ground. Downhill sections of equal steepness had the rear tire slide while I gentled the front brake. Such slow going convinced me it might have been faster to walk. Though I was somewhat enjoying myself, the first 20 miles of this terrain took four hours.

After cresting another of many first gear climbs I edged around a corner and saw that a rural bus had left the road. People there told me that the bus, while going down the slope too fast, met an equally too-fast jeep at the narrow crossing. The bus driver swerved and stopped with the right front wheel in a muddy stream, the left front off the tree-limb bridge and neither rear wheel able to get traction. Concurrently the jeep ripped off a portion of the wooden bus body. This happened the day before and stranded the passengers without food or water.

The men added logs to the ravine crossing to make it safe for the bike to pass. Then even more logs were tossed on top of the pile and the bus extracted from its muddy pit.

Traffic that had stopped to help totaled three jeeps, a pair of oxen and one motorcycle after I arrived. The crossing had been torn up by the accident and more logs were laid so the bike could pass. After a picture everyone stopped work to watch me climb the next hill to park. I shed excess clothing, took more pictures and went back to help push the bus back onto the road. Two of the jeeps were tied together then both were tied to the bus. A stout man, who weighed about 250 pounds, sat in the lead jeep to give its tires more traction. We bent shoulders to the bus, the jeeps backed up and heave-ho we moved it not a bit. There was more shoveling of mud and shifting of planks under tires and on our second try the front was freed. More digging and plank placing restored the bus for a self-powered assault on the grade ahead. Oxen were goaded out of the way, jeeps scattered into the underbrush and the BSA was moved ahead.

Then the bus groaned up the grade amid "Bravos" from its sweaty saviors. I certainly didn't want to follow such a slow train so it was quick in the saddle to be first off along the ruts. About a half mile farther the passengers were waiting in the shade of overhanging trees. Privatation was evident with crying children and worried women vocally thankful for news that the bus was out and should be along shortly.

In a short time the ruts became somewhat user-friendly and jungle underbrush gave way to small plantations of sugar cane surrounding grass huts. Riding was so good, comparatively, that I became careless on a steep hill and hung the crankcase on a projecting log. A bit later the roadway became smooth all the way into the village of La Cruz where I was directed to another frontier control station. Officers inspected luggage, stamped me into the country and said that lunch could be found "that way."

The two men worked for the U.S. InterAmerican Geodetic Survey project which had become active in mapping much of Latin America after WW II was over.

The combination post office, grocery store, cantina, feed store, gas station and lunch room was hosting the Costa Rican travelers and two Americans working for our Inter-American Geodetic Survey. Before I could sit down the Americans cheerfully explained that the easy portion of the route had been completed. Ahead, between me and San Jose, there were no fewer than 20 rivers, some of which were "that" wide and six to eight feet deep. One of the Americans seriously recommended a ride back to Nicaragua and shipping the bike and me to Costa Rica by boat. Not realizing what was ahead, I said, "Thank you very much" and ordered lunch. It was great: chicken and rice soup with huge chunks of chicken, steak, roast beef with rice and beans, hot pepper sauce, fresh corn, fresh butter for the rolls, a sweet corn drink called Chi Chi and fruit for desert.

My fellow travelers were long gone before I left La Cruz. The road, as it could have been called, now passed over flat land embellished with a plentiful supply of good-size rocks eager to break an unsuspecting crankcase with the greatest of ease. Many of them were hidden under powderlike dust, which sprayed from the front wheel like water. Unlike water it plugged nostrils, grimed sweaty hands and itched fearfully under the collar of my riding suit. A narrow river was a welcome change from the dust and fording was accomplished without incident. This increased my confidence at the next, much wider, expanse of running water. Wading disclosed no unusual potential problems so it was back to the bike for what seemed destined to be a successful fording. The shallow entrance was smooth and splashing through the cooling water great fun until I hung up on a largish rock near mid-stream. Keeping the engine running while it fed the submerged exhaust pipe was no chore. By swinging on the bars I freed the front wheel and cautiously started off. About ten feet further the ford deepened and revealed the engine's inability to function with a spark plug submerged under water. It was a disgusting feeling to be stranded in the middle of another river with not a helpful soul in site.

My silent debate as to the most appropriate action was interrupted by nearby laughter. Turning around I almost bumped my head against a curious horse. Apparently its smiling rider had followed me into the river while enjoying my struggles and final defeat. I couldn't help but laugh with him until we calmed down to discuss the value of a lariat being tied to the steering damper so the horse could pull me to dry land. It worked and after assurances that the engine would start in a few minutes my new friend waved *adios* and rode away. The ignition dried, the engine kickstarted and we thumped off through more dust.

Shortly afterward I turned left instead of right and found myself inside an isolated cow pasture. The farmer appeared and led me though a horse pen toward the route to Liberia where I intended to spend the night. About a quarter-mile further on the thick dust had carefully hidden a huge chuck hole into which I proceeded to bury the front wheel, hang up on the case and hear the rear tire spin in naked air. Dismount, tug the beast to a rideable condition and continue. Soon afterward an oncoming jeep driver on his way to Nicaragua stopped for a few minutes to give me the most vital information of all. "Always take the right turn if there's any doubt as to which path is the proper way," he

Though this river was deep, the bottom was smooth enough that the horse had little trouble pulling me out.

advised. His recommendation was priceless as almost immediately forks became more numerous with better appearing ruts leading left.

My overnight in Liberia was made easier by finding a member of the *Guardia Civil* which was both police and army in rural areas. While talking with him I noticed that rust prevention techniques included a rod of wood and an oiled rag driven into the muzzle of his rifle, a greased rag wadded in the chamber where it was held in place by the bolt and cartridges wrapped in oiled

There was no connection between this hotel and that in Nicaragua. Here there was a decent bed, good food and a water well far distant from the outhouse.

Even this shallow section of the river
was too deep and the water is almost above
tops of the tires and well over the spark plug.

rags inside his belt loops. The soldier-policeman directed me to the Hotel Rivas which was the only hotel in town. The room with meals was ₡ 9 (*colones*) ($1.10 U.S.) and check-in was at 5:45 P.M. which meant an average of ten miles an hour for the afternoon. After my shower and dinner the bike was moved into the dining patio to re-fit the muffler, which had loosened during one of the day's many hang-ups. Benches in front of the hotel were comfortable and I joined a few of the other guests. One of them, a truck driver, offered transportation through the next day's rivers, which he assured me were the deepest of any on the road. Several youths suggested attendance at the village dance and said the girls were as pretty as those in the States. It all sounded wonderful, as did music of a nearby Marimba band, but I was pooped and bed was the best idea of them all.

Breakfast Monday morning was a community affair with three truck drivers at the table. Each tried to outdo the other two with horrendous details of the road to San Jose but discounting their stories provided a reasonable idea of the future which was considered possible. A $10 American banknote was exchanged for 75 *colones*, the hotel bill paid and gas and oil were topped up at the only station. Out-of-town smooth dirt lasted about a mile to banks of the granddaddy of them all. A water-way that seemed about 300 feet wide, running both smooth and deep, and where was that truck driver with his free ride to San Jose?

A walkover proved one thing. It was much too deep to ride through under power. But there was no help in sight and I decided there was a better chance of being towed out of the river than if parked on the bank thumbing a lift. I fired up the engine and splashed into the water, which was running so fast the only way to keep the bike upright was to point the front wheel more or less upstream. Finally the water became deeper, was over the spark plug and again we were out of business. No laughing horseman this time. Only the busy churning of river water trying to push the bike over.

I eased the prop stand down then used a spare foot to push stones under the stand so everything would remain reasonably upright. After dismounting, several large rocks were shoved against both tires on the downstream side to keep the bike from washing away. I splashed back to dry land to take pictures then sat in the shade of a nearby tree. Water was still draining from my boots when three men arrived on very healthy horses. After a bit of jesting about my problem the leader of the group was agreeable to giving me a tow but was not sure it would be successful. The bike's weight was verbally underestimated and he was told about a "much smaller horse" that had provided help the day before. After we moved into the river his rope was looped firmly and the horse braced for a pull when a sudden gust of wind blew his hat into the water. He dropped his end of the rope and all three horsemen chased downstream after the rapidly floating headgear.

They caught the hat and returned, laughing about a sopping hat and water-logged motorcycle rider, to where I was waiting in the river. With the first pull it was obvious that weight of the bike, plus towing it over the rocky bottom through deep water, was a heavy trip and the poor horse staggered several times before we made dry land. Meanwhile the youngest of the trio had ridden back to the other side, picked up my belongings and brought them to me. An offer of payment was totally rejected as the men expressed greater interest in knowing if I would be able to restart and make it to the next next town. I convinced them of my eventual success and they rode away with friendly waves.

While the bike was drying out the Costa Rican party navigated their way across the river in an area that seemed a bit less deep than the route I had tried.

The magneto was decapped and the spark plug wire removed so they could dry while I sat on a handy boulder draining my boots again. This operation was in progress when a vehicle horn sounded from the other bank and the Costa Ricans shouted questions about the water's depth. I measured it from the ground for them and their Land Rover bounced into the ford. About halfway over one of the men splashed off the back to paddle in the cool water. On my side of the river we compared notes of the road and I learned that this was the last large river. From now one the going would get progressively better. They said! By now the swimmer had returned and they left after my solemn assurance that everything would be running in a few minutes. But solemn assurance failed to impress the engine as 15 minutes of drying and dropping on the kickstarter did nothing but make me sweat. Finally the beast gave up in disgust and broke into a roar when I jumped on the kickstarter for the dozenth time.

The dirt was good and in another mile I arrived at a shallow but broad strip of water, which to be on the safe side, was inspected carefully. The passageway seemed OK but there was no compression and the kickstarter spun the engine as though it were a child's top. The diagnosis was that sudden chilling of the block in the previous stream plus heating from the short ride had warped a valve. For some happy reason the valve surrendered after resting a few minutes and the engine started with heartwarming racket.

On the other side of this easy ford the road was nice gravel into the village of Las Cañas. My Costa Rican friends had mentioned a good hotel at which to eat. When I found it there was a place at the table for me. We enjoyed lunch while they offered a wealth of encouraging information about the road ahead.

Even the bike found it difficult to find an easy pathway through this typical collection of case-busters.

This better-than-usual section of the Interamerican Highway made riding a pleasure after the hours of frequent rivers and unfriendly large rocks.

The dirt was in fact excellent for about ten miles. Then it became what could be considered another "worst" section that was narrow, twisty and rutted with more of the fine dust which sprayed into my face when I rode too fast. Headsize rocks hid under the same pulverized earth and one of them reared up and tore the spring loose from the prop stand. The driver of a nearby truck used his coffee-break time and tools to help me fix it. I was absolutely beat after a few more miles of this commotion and stopped at each of several small streams to wash and cool my hands and face. After a slip of the front wheel against a hidden rock disconnected the muffler, it dangled until a shade tree arrived under which to park. Refitting was completed when a bull showed up. Irritated by noise from the restarted engine, he chased me vigorously for a few hundred feet before giving up.

After more dirt and sweat I found the Costa Rican party, which had waited by a short cut that would cost only ₡2 (25¢ U.S.). By now spending money on a better road seemed like a good idea. We bounced up to a double-padlocked gate where a non-descript individual collected the toll and waved us on. The ups and downs of his toll road were steeper than the "highway" but not so dusty. After a mile of this we were back on the main road. The helpful truck driver had bypassed us and my friends apologized for leading me off on a goose chase.

A length of fairly good dirt, which was a completed section of *La Carretera Interamericana*, led into the village of Esparta for a cold drink. A review of time and mileage disclosed that it had taken over seven hours to travel 90 miles, 54 of which had been ridden in two hours. From Esparta to San Ramón was an hour-long ride up into mountains where my teeth chattered and the leather jacket felt good. In San Ramón (7069 miles) an English-speaking druggist, whose son had graduated from Ohio State, provided direction to the best hotel, which was some distance away. One of the town kids volunteered to guide me. He was planted on the hard tank to the merriment of his friends who thought he was sitting on a man's lap. Their laughter, and his, changed when we took off at full throttle. I thought the kid was going to break my arms as he held on for his thrill of the year. The hotel was a typical Latin pension which charged ₡7.25 (95¢ U.S.) for dinner, room overnight and breakfast. Dinner consisted of soup, two fried eggs, bread, potatoes, rice, beans, steak, spiced cauliflower and fried bananas, with pears and coffee for desert.

The next day's run from San Ramón to San Jose was over paved roads with unmarked curves, slippery oxen calling cards and few direction signs at crossings. The road branched more often than the map so inquiries were the order of the morning. Locals gave interesting responses when asked for direction to San Jose their capital city. You could almost hear their wheels turning with "It's thataway where it's been as long as I can remember."

Outside San Jose a traffic policeman wanted to inspect my driver's license. I explained that none was available as I hadn't arrived yet and here was my passport to prove it. After he believed I had ridden from Nicaragua my stock went up about 50 percent and he waved me on with a snappy salute for good luck. I was, as usual, completely lost because the highway map had no city street section. Direction from a pushcart peddler helped and an errand boy pointed me to the Pension Canada two blocks away. Charley Balzer, the owner, took one look at a tattered motorcycle rider and gave me the dungeon, a basement room. I squawked and he found upstairs quarters across from a bath I had all to myself.

Selfish soaking in my first tubbing for over two weeks drained the pension's hot-water tank and I didn't even feel guilty. Later Charley produced a terrific meal and sent my suit out with promises of prompt cleaning and pressing. That afternoon I rode to the American Embassy for letters and to the post office for a registered parcel I'd sent myself from Honduras. After waiting in the proper line the girl clerk said I couldn't get the parcel because I needed a passport for identification. I had left mine at the pension. That was no problem, only a few minutes ride, which turned out to be idle thinking as the engine was again completely without compression. I spun it until sweat poured but to no avail. A nearby lunch counter provided a glass of milk and dry cake while my brow cooled. This didn't impress the bike and subsequent attempts to start the beast created little more than muscle ache from exertion. The telephone book gave me a number and a long explanation convinced an unknown BSA motorcycle dealer to move the beast into his shop for inspection and repairs.

Retrieving the bike the next morning was something of a problem as no one in the pension knew just exactly where the shop address was situated. Walking around San Jose provided plenty of exercise until, after about two hours of searching, Cyclo-Sport was found near the main public market. In the backshop a mechanic was fussing with the BSA's magneto while another was checking for loose nuts and bolts. The owner, Tiberia Paganelli, an Italian who had been in Costa Rica for 25 years, greeted me as a long lost friend and wanted to know all about the journey. And most importantly, "How did the BSA hold up?" His clients were wandering in and out to look the machine over and I've long wondered how many he sold on the strength of recommendations I was giving. They had the engine running when I asked for the bill. There was none. "A courtesy of the house and thank you for stopping."

My subsequent visit to Costa Rica was somewhat divided into four parts. Article research at the Inter-American Agricultural Institute at Turrialba, writing about the Costa Rica Northern Railway to Puerto Limón, preparing a story on the government's electric railroad to Puntarenas and enjoying one very fine visit to the city of San Jose. This latter activity included local riders finding time to guide me throughout the countryside to visit special points of interest.

In El Salvador I had been given a letter of introduction to the secretary to the president of Costa Rica, so bright and early one morning I'm in the presidential office building with my letter. The page was well-dressed in a tailored suit but his brains must have been left at home. He accepted the letter, told me he would take care of it and (as I discovered later) dropped it into the incoming mail basket. Two hours later he asked why I was still there. I explained, the security guard gave him hell and a few minutes later I had my audience. The secretary was most apologetic about my long wait and offered every assistance. My plans to write magazine articles about railroads and the Turrialba Institute generated handsomely engraved cards introducing me to the executive officer of each organization.

The next project was to obtain a Costa Rica motorcycle license plate for my collection. At the *Departmento de Transito, Guardia Civil* my explanation was going well until one of the desk officers began to throw questions faster than I could understand. A local attorney waiting nearby gave me his business card and became a much-appreciated interpreter who detailed my needs in a more complete fashion.

The Pension Canada was not too sharp from the outside but the food was great, the room and bath clean and many guests were Americans from the Canal Zone.

With my request now adequately explained the desk officer became ready and willing to help. The office for license plate issuing was next door and if I would care to step over they would be glad to take care of me. There I met the chief of registration who evidenced pleasure at meeting one so mad as to ride a motorcycle from California and would I be so kind as to overlook that he had not shaved that morning. This was easily forgiven as he was holding a new motorcycle plate in his hand for which I had only to sign a receipt.

Correspondence and draft-notes for the magazine articles called for a typewriter. The first store I visited would be glad to rent one for ₡25 ($3 U.S.) a month but unfortunately their only rental unit was in the repair shop and no one knew when it would be back. The second typewriter shop had no rentals but sent me several blocks to a repair man who was supposed to have rentals. He displayed a beatup old

Ten miles from San Jose, trains of the Northern cross the Continental Divide which is 1539 meters above sea level at this point.

Underwood which had been checked over and could be had for ₡25 for 30 days. That evening he arrived at the pension with the machine under his arm and a receipt billing me ₡75 ($9) instead of the ₡25 quoted. I told him to forget it and take the thing home. That made some difference and the rental became ₡50 for the month. After I decided it would be at the original price or not at all, it was not at all and the man left with the Underwood. The following morning, acting on what proved to be a good guess, I rechecked the first store, which had a machine out for repairs. Good news. Their machine had been returned and could be rented. That evening the store's delivery boy arrived with the same typewriter the repairman had shown me the night before!

Writing an article about the Costa Rica Northern Railway began on a Monday when I reported to offices of the line in San Jose. After introductions the operations manager, Harold Averre, walked me through the freight yard to a gasoline-powered railcar. We chugged out onto the main line for three hours of railroading over the Continental Divide, through picturesque canyons and along the Reventazón River to arrive at Loma and the temporary "Tunnel Station." This was as far as tracked equipment could go because two months previously the rail line had suffered the world's largest landslide. A movement of earth over three-fourths of a mile wide and two miles long had covered track and right-of-way with mud and rock to a depth of as much as 100 feet, destroyed a valley of grazing meadow and forced the mighty Reventazón River to change its course. Leaving the railcar at the face of the slide we hiked over the mass of destruction with Charles Riggs, the line's construction engineer. I had never before visited such a major construction project so when someone shouted "Fire" I didn't duck. There was a tremendous upheaval of dirt and the earth shook as dynamite blasted a portion of the slide away. I shook too as a fist-size chunk of rock smashed into the ground about three feet away.

While on a flight to Puerto Limón the pilot flew over the landslide which can be seen as the misplaced land above and right of the propeller spinner.

From San Jose this was as far as trains could travel because track to the right was buried under the two-mile-long landslide along the Reventazón river.

Averre gave me a dirty look for being so dumb as to stand in a direct line with the blast and decided it would be safer if we all had something to eat. The cook had not expected guests so our fare was somewhat on the crude side; thick black coffee, mammoth slices of unsalted white bread and a glob of soft black beans to spread between the slices. Following lunch I took pictures of the devastated area before the two executives escorted me to another railcar for travel to the far end of the line at Puerto Limón. After we rattled out of the spectacular mountain area the jungle-like landscape hosted an occasional banana or cacao plantation, or small village. We made no stops and arrived in Puerto Limón's main yards about dusk. The railcar switched onto trackage along a city street to reach the local railroad offices from where I was escorted to the company's guest house. It was a cozy four-bedroom cottage complete with a black housekeeper who had dinner on the table a few minutes after I arrived.

Because it was not possible to get heavy machinery onto the landslide site, rubble had to be carried away rock by rock before a new roadbed could be built.

Transportation from the landslide site to Puerto Limón was behind the front section of a Model A Ford powering a locally-constructed railcar.

Machine shops of the Northern could completely rebuild steam locomotives, railroad cars and construct heavy maintenance equipment.

No. 11, one of the Northern's active locomotives, was nearly 100 years old and said to function well as the result of its many scheduled rebuildings.

The casket was loaded into the funeral car while friends of the family waited in passenger coaches for their journey to the cemetery.

Tuesday was a busy day. After introductions to the staff I toured and photographed the machine shops, took pictures of working engines built in 1897, visited a very modern foundry and watched the cutting of ties and construction of box cars from local components. A novel feature of the Northern's Limón yards was a long shallow dip-tank with rails along the bottom. As rolling stock was pushed through the two-foot depth of diesel oil the wheels and trucks would be coated to slow down the formation of rust. While photographing I heard talk of a funeral train scheduled to operate later that afternoon and requested permission to ride along. One of the men said he would inquire for me.

The bereaved family did not object and I boarded the train at five that afternoon. A locomotive and tender had been coupled to a sparkling white funeral car which was about half the length of box cars I had seen elsewhere on the line. Its doors had been removed and a raised dais constructed in the center of the car to support the casket in plain view. Benches were attached to the car's inside walls as seating for the family and close friends. Behind the funeral car were passenger coaches for friends.

The section of the cemetery on the far side of the tracks, for the less affluent, is where rocks were layered on coffins to keep them from floating on high-level groundwater.

The train waited quietly while the widow, two daughters and the family dog were last to leave the gravesite.

I rode on the platform of the last coach as the train backed along a city street and stopped by a church. Soon the church doors opened and mourners poured out to follow the casket as it was carried to the waiting train and lifted into the funeral car. The black family and its relatives took their seats, friends were in the coaches and the train returned to the station where the engineer was given his orders. Then we moved onto the line toward the cemetery to which there was no usable vehicle road.

All the women wore white, the men wore black, the children white and Carroll had on a white shirt and dark trousers. There was little conversation in the coaches during travel to the burial ground. The major activity was the family dog sniffing along the coach aisle seeking a place to urinate. When we arrived the train stopped on the main line. After the passengers and casket were off, the engine and empty cars moved ahead onto a siding. Halfway up the trackside hill the casket was placed on a mound

San Jose offices of the government's electric railroad to the Pacific coast were being painted.

of fresh earth and surrounded by mourners. A young minister read the service in English, the widow cried and eight little girls clutched floral offerings while huddled together, shifty-eyed and obviously uncomfortable.

After the service was completed the undertaker and his helper removed the metal casket handles so they could be used again and threaded two worn manila ropes under the box. Lowering it into the ground was quick but the sound of rough rope being withdrawn from under the box sent shudders up my spine. The widow's clod of earth bounced and echoed off the flimsy lid. Others followed and everyone seemed relieved when enough dirt had been thrown in to stop echoes from the half-empty box. Pallbearers took turns shoveling fill dirt and when they tired younger friends of the family did their bit. Soon the mound was completed. The eight bug-eyed little girls hastily tossed their flowers on the fresh soil and ran away toward the tracks. There was little conversation while mourners walked back to the train but once it was in motion, "Let's be cheerful now" was the order of the day. Children laughed and played again, youths made private jokes and their elders joyously sang hymns from their church books. Even the dog seemed happier while chasing his obviously numerous fleas.

I was up at four the next morning to catch the six o'clock train, The first person I met in the coach was a white Angelican minister on his way to the interior to care for widespread members of his all-black flock.

From him I learned something of the trials and tribulations of a missionary. Such as children who defiled his church for want of something to do, young adults who found it a convenient place for fornication and older parishioners who resented the intrusion of a foreigner. The poor man said he had to fight, and whip, one of the city toughs to get his congregation started. But in four years he had increased it from 60 to over 300 churchgoers.

The minister and I happened to observe one of the more unfortunate situations of life. Occupying the seat ahead was a lovely Costa Rican girl traveling to visit her sick father. Single men in the coach tried to cheer her up with cold drinks and encouraged her to have a few swallows from their community brandy bottle. She was well relaxed by the time she neared her destination and no longer obviously sorrowed over her father's illness. When the train stopped one of the men carried her bag to the station and was nearby when a sister rushed up with sad tidings. Their father had died that morning. As the train pulled out the two girls were embracing in shade of the station's overhanging roof, weeping on each other's shoulder while naked children and pigs clustered for comfort in the same shade.

My other railroad article was about the Government-owned *Ferrocarril Electrico Al Pacifico* which runs to the Pacific Ocean. I met with the director of public works, who turned me over to the secretary of the railroad who passed me down to the master mechanic who was the best person to help anyhow. On the first day I toured and photographed their large and modern workshop where, in one corner of the building, there was a Catholic altar at which most of the shop personnel worshipped on Sunday. The following day I spent the morning photographing rolling stock and rail yard installations. When I returned after lunch to shoot the power house the secretary said, "No go." Locals, not happy with their government, had bombed the plant. Although the explosion did little damage he thought that nervousness of the guards might cause me trouble. I agreed and arranged to visit the railroad's Pacific terminus at Puntarenas, another major Costa Rican port.

An unusual feature in workshops of the government's railroad was this altar before which Sunday services are held for the trainmen and families.

Skilled Costa Rican workmen constructed much of their railroad's rolling stock such as this combination passenger/freight coach.

That following day included riding in a coach all morning and photographing sites along the railway. In Puntarenas the yardmaster arranged for me to travel in the electric locomotive of the returning train. The engineer took time to explain the controls and the brakeman shared his lunch. There was more photography and in one very scenic spot the train was stopped so I could get a better shot. Later that afternoon I transferred into the baggage car and rode in the cupola with one of the brakemen.

Horsedrawn wagons were common in freight yards of the electric line. The wheelbarrow and shovel were to clean up afterward.

When the Puntarenas train stopped on the main street of this town it was besieged by vendors with hot food, fresh fruit and cold drinks.

As the train was rushing through a lowland jungle area the engineer slammed on the brakes and we grabbed for anything solid as train wheels slid to a stop. From our cupola we watched the engineer jump from his cab and run back toward the conductor while shouting like a madman. The conductor was shouting back, "*Si, Si, Si.*" ("Yes, Yes, Yes") The two separated, reboarded and the train was backed rapidly until we stopped with our empty box car spotted near people emerging from the jungle. Someone told me that a woman of an interior village had taken sick. She had been loaded on an old canvas cot and carried for several miles to the railroad tracks for transportation to the government hospital in San Jose. The box car was opened, half a village climbed in with the ill woman and we lurched off again. Darkness fell and from the cupola I watched long blue sparks fly off the engine's trolley and smash against the window in front of my face. We had become a ghost train rushing through the night while chasing bright energies of a mystic being. On our arrival in San Jose an ambulance from the hospital met the train and in the excitement I slipped quietly away to find a taxi for a ride to the pension.

49 Kilometers outside of San Jose, Extra Train No. 3 stopped to pick up this sick women for transportation to the hospital.

The Turrialba project involved
teaching modern agricultural techniques to farmers
living in the tropical climatic zones of Costa Rica.

My third project in Cost Rica was an article about the Inter-American Institute of Agricultural Sciences in Turrialba. A three-day visit to the institute took care of interviews and gave me time to inspect educational programs in nearby villages. Turrialba appeared to be a fine project but, unfortunately, like most good work it was not very interesting and no article was written. The day after I returned from Turrialba, a pair of French girls arrived at the pension on their drive from California to Venezuela. Both had jobs waiting for them in South America and were were having a wonderful time. Renate, the elder of the two, was a trim blond who spoke Spanish like a native and wasn't to be taken by anyone. The younger girl, Suzanne, was a bit on the plump side and somewhat shy. We talked a little but they were off on a different track and we seldom saw each other.

Near the end of my stay in Costa Rica, after visiting the embassy for mail, a traffic policeman wanted to inspect my driver's license. Of course I had none and though I was leaving in a few days he insisted that a license be obtained. Because it cost nothing I didn't object. When it was time to pump up the bike and carry us to his office the engine wouldn't start. After several minutes of my jumping on the kickstarter the officer suggested that, because it was near his lunch time, would I mind returning to the same street corner after two o'clock so we could go to the police station together? He disappeared and the engine started. After lunch we met as promised and he rode the rear fender to an *Officina de Transito* where an officer expressed interest in my trip, issued a yellow slip good for eight days of driving in Costa Rica and wished me well.

Leaving San Jose (7354 miles) wasn't as simple as it sounds. My visitor's permit had expired by three days and before departure the fee of ₡15 ($2) was paid for another tax stamp. Then I started for Puntarenas where I had been a week before on the train. There was good pavement to Palmares followed by new construction gravel and graveled dirt the rest of the way. In Puntarenas I looked for the yardmaster who had arranged my ride in the electric locomotive, to inquire about lodgings. However he had been transferred to San Jose and the new man didn't know me from Adam's off ox. The railroad porter led me along the sidewalk to the only hotel, which was easier riding than on the sand streets. A policeman objected to bike tires on the narrow paving and gave me hell. "Why don't you use the street like other self-respecting drivers?" he wanted to know.

When I reached the hotel and rode into the lobby the manager was so amused by the mechanical intrusion that he gave me the lowest commercial room rate. Like ₡15 ($2) for meals and a bed for the night.

The people of Costa Rica were highly literate and bilingual advertising and direction signs were common.

We mutually agreed to roll the bike onto the front porch and were doing great until a rotted flooring plank gave way and dropped its heavy end onto the crankcase. After laughs at my embarrassment other guests helped lift the rear onto solid footing. A few minutes later the hotel's owner returned with hammer and saw in hand to repair the damage.

My upstairs room was typically tropical: an iron bed with scaling white paint, leaning walls, peeling wallpaper and a magnificent view of the Pacific ocean through a grove of palm trees. The bathroom at the far end of the hotel demonstrated that toilet walls do not have to be abused by bad jokes or poetry. In Puntarenas it was political candidates who were on the walls with a thorough going-over including graphic references to their manliness or lack of same.

Among my dinner companions that night there was a ranch owner planning a trip around the world who couldn't find anyone to go with him and the captain of a coastal launch who fell asleep every few minutes because he had been working all the previous night and day. The youngest diner was nine years old, Hindu dark with the features of an Englishman. He had three years of schooling and could speak passable English from association with crewmen of ships which had harbored at Puntarenas. He wanted to learn more English so that when he became stronger he could work on American fishing boats for ₡15 ($2 U.S.) a day, which he said would be very good wages.

With all good humor the Puntarenas' hotel owner fixed the porch floor where the bike had dropped through the planking.

Loading in the morning included web-strapping the metal case and its rubber pad over the waterproof war-surplus ammunition cases bolted onto the rear fender.

Sleep was not easy that night as the adjacent house of pleasure began to jump about the time I sacked in. A bed-shaking earthquake at six in the morning almost tossed me out of bed and continued rattling the walls as I rushed to the balcony in search of information. What a disappointment. A train of freight cars was lurching along tracks by the front of the hotel. There was no use trying for more sleep so it was off to breakfast which was foul. Three eggs were gamey, the orange over-ripe and toast three days old. Coffee was unmentionable.

I walked the town and exchanged money during the morning hours. At first the bank clerk was not interested in giving me the official rate of exchange but after I complained he and the manager agreed to give me ₡7.40 for each dollar. A coffee-grower who was also staying in the hotel offered a visit through the dock-side warehouse where his coffee beans were being repacked. On its way to town the truck-load of coffee had overturned in a river. Drying the coffee was no problem but every sack was ruined. Warehouse laborers, at ₡5 (70¢ U.S.) a

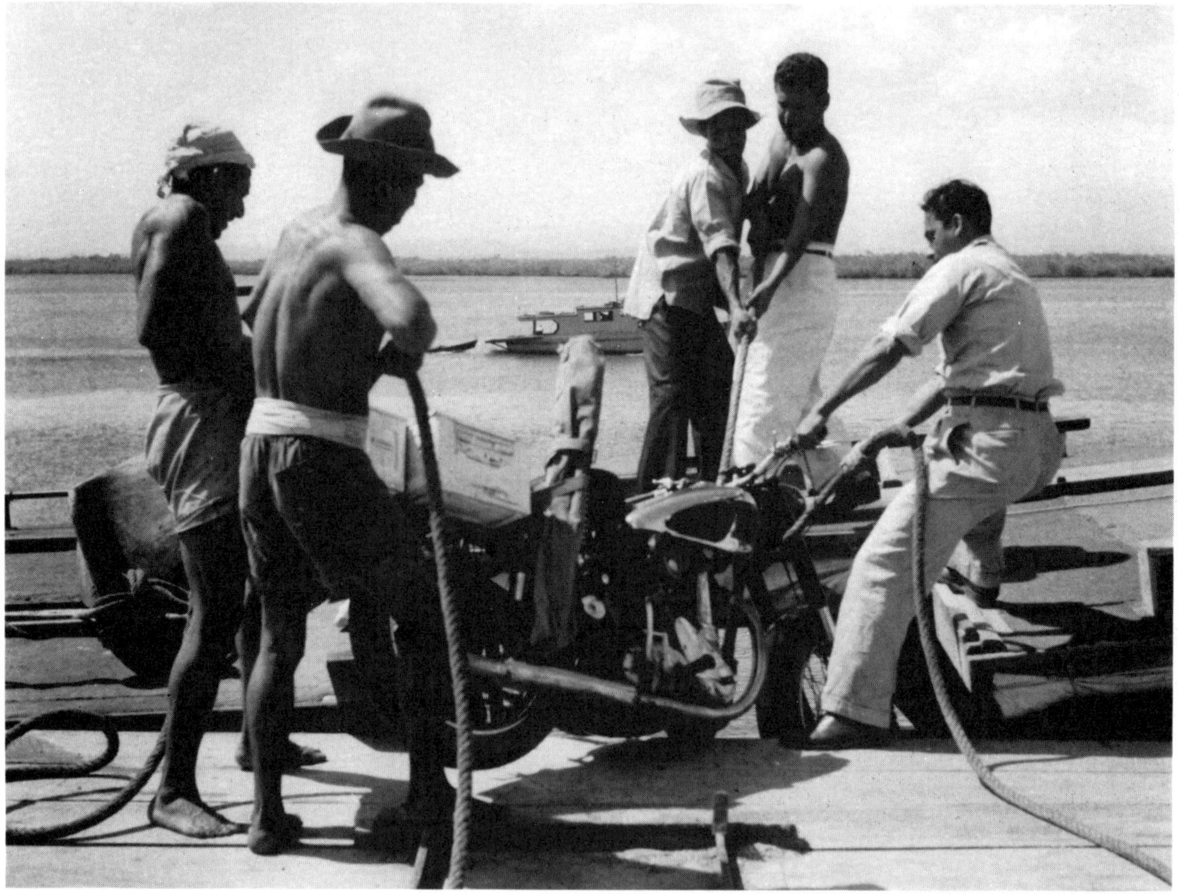

Five sturdy men and two lengths of rope lowered the BSA onto the deck of the coastal launch docked at the wharf in Puntarenas.

day, were transferring the raw coffee beans from water-damaged sacks to new sacks, stenciling the grower's name and address on the side and marking some sacks "A" and others "B." The grower told me that of all coffee produced, a specified percentage (A vs. B) must remain in Costa Rica for local consumption.

After lunch I checked out of the hotel to board a Pacific coastal launch for a ride from Puntarenas to Puerto Cortes near the southern end of Costa Rica. The fares, paid in San Jose, were ₡15 ($2 U.S.) to reserve my 16-hour voyage on the *Santa Cruz*, plus ₡25 ($3 U.S.) for the bike and luggage. From Puerto Cortes there were railroads into Panama but no roads. Accordingly the launch trip was the only way I could get around the area of "no roads/no way" past San Ysidro de General in the mountain heights of *Cordillera de Talamanca.*

To reach the launch I rode through the busy coffee-bagging warehouse, onto the wharf, bumped over its railroad tracks and continued to the ocean end where the *Santa Cruz* was docked. Loading the bike began as soon as my luggage was untied. Five men wrapped thick ropes about the machine, picked it up and lowered it gently onto the deck where it was rolled to the bow for the overnight voyage.

Crewmen of the Santa Cruz
had to try the saddle, twist the throttle
and apparently dream of owning their own bike.

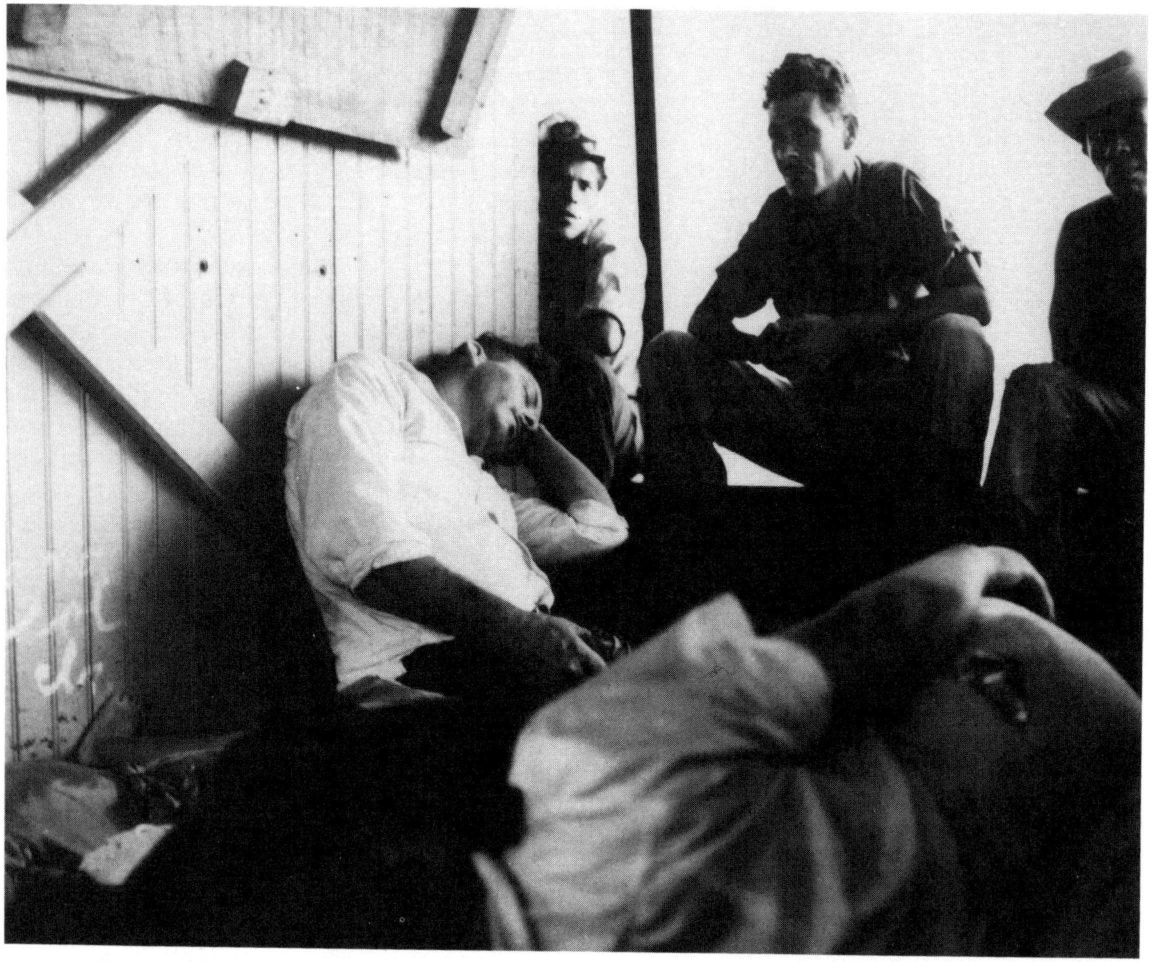

Decks of the Santa Cruz were covered with sleeping bodies when I woke after the morning sun began to brighten the ocean haze.

In addition to one motorcycle; the launch carried school desks, 300-pound chunks of ice in burlap bags with rice hulls for insulation, metal drain spouts, fresh fruits, canned goods, three parrots, three Belgian nationals, ten children and 35 Costa Ricans who argued loudly while staking out a portion of the deck or bench on which to sleep. Soon we were all on board and the launch rode well as it cleared customs and chugged out into the Pacific. It was smooth sailing at first and I photographed the breakwater, Puntarenas from the ocean side and saw the hulks of two Italian freighters that had decorated harbor waters since early days of WW II. Both ships had steamed into Puntarenas about the time that Costa Rica declared war on the Axis powers. Rather than surrender their vessels, the captains decided to scuttle them and submerge their valuable cargoes of marble under waters of the harbor.

By mid-afternoon the ocean was no longer smooth and the little launch hiked up one side and down the other of impressive waves. Two hours of this and the *Santa Rosa* hove into view. As it belonged to the same maritime line the two craft halted while their crews discussed attributes of the one pretty girl we had on board. Once they completed their discussion to everyone's satisfaction, including that of the flattered girl, we resumed travel. Our crew members hung fishing lines overboard and made a strike, but the five-pounder was a disappointment. Passengers who had moved out of the fishing area to avoid being wet by the wiggling fish didn't have time to return to their seats before another line began to jump. This time a 12-pound fighting barracuda was gaffed and cleaned within minutes. Too big for the ice chest, it was shoved under a seat.

Sunset over the Pacific was a colorful experience with a mountain's exposed soil reflecting an amber glow across the waves. Darkness fell, launch lights were turned on and dinner was served. Steaks, fish, coffee and bread. I asked for the same meal the crew ate, which turned out to be fried pork-like patties between chunks of white bread with powerful coffee to hold it down. Children who had been put to sleep, when the voyage began, drowsed on deck hatches. Many parents woke only long enough to eat and roll over to resume snoozing.

My bed on a bench was about a foot wide and short enough for my feet to hang over the end. Using the camera bag for a pillow, and finding a soft spot on its mechanical contents, was a lost cause until I dozed off and forgot all about the metal lump under my head. Once I awoke and looked up to a wonderful skyful of stars, which swayed back and forth in wavelike rhythm as though the launch was not moving but the sky was. Later I turned over and found the dead fish staring me in the face. Its glassy eyes were disturbing and I shoved the creature along the deck to bother someone else.

About five in the morning false dawn arrived and nature called. A visit to the head included stepping carefully among sleeping bodies wedged shoulder to shoulder on the swaying deck. In the lavatory everything was going fine until the launch changed direction and crested huge seas. As the little room tossed and pitched the throne valve leaked with a rush and I was almost drowned (backwards) while sitting on a geyser. I grabbed the towel bar as it sailed by at the same time the throne disappeared downward. The launch changed direction. The toilet came up and I came down to smack the wooden seat so hard my teeth chattered.

Then up again. Bang. Down again. I braced myself between the door and washbowl, pulled zippers in all directions at once and got out of the closet before I was beaten to death.

As we neared coastal waters the ocean quieted and I backed the engineers into a corner to learn more about their maritime service. They told me the *Santa Cruz* carried a captain, pilot, two engineers, a cook and three seamen on its twice-a-week round trips between Puntarenas and Puerto Cortes. One of the engineers pointed back over the stern where for the first time I saw another launch. It was the *Filadelphia*, which had followed us all night as she carried no pilot.

Breakfast was announced but there were few takers. Many passengers appeared ill, a few hardy souls remained asleep, some were eating fruit from brown bags and I was cautious. One of the three parrots was small, hungry and apparently very nearsighted.

It was walking around a hatch cover when it bumped into a bigger parrot. The large bird was as seasick as any bird could be and hadn't taken a step for at least an hour. Its only movement was to sway slowly to compensate for motion of the launch. Not being able to see too well, the little parrot must have thought, "Food at last and green leaves at that." So up to the big parrot the little one went and pulled out a feather. The feather was spit away so promptly it must have tasted terrible.

The little bird hopped around behind the big parrot and yanked out a tail feather. And spit it away in equally evident disgust. More hopping brought the hungry one around to the front again and another breast feather was pulled. By this time most of us were laughing and wondering aloud how dumb the big parrot was. Our entertainment program was canceled by the owner of all three birds. He dropped the hungry little fellow into a paper bag and tossed in a chunk of bread for the parrot to chew on.

The Filadelphia has entered the straits and follows us along the coast to the river leading inland to Puerto Cortes.

After our pilot set a diagonal course toward the deserted coastline the more experienced passengers busied themselves with collecting belongings and re-tying luggage. An engineer told me that in a few minutes we would ride through the breakers and over a sand bar, then cruise south along the coast toward the mouth of the Rio Diquis, which we would follow upstream to Puerto Cortes. From my point of view the breakers ahead appeared much too dangerous and neither could I see a river. The crewman assured me that such navigation was routine, they always went through the breakers and not very often did the launch tip over. This was the best he could do before hurrying below deck to join his partner in the engine room.

At a point where the surf seemed highest, and the coast nearest, the bow of the launch was pointed shoreward. Up in mid air we rose on the first crest, then slammed down as the wave rolled by. The engine roared faster and we rode the crest of another mound of water, which carried us over the sand bar and almost to shore. The engine shut down and the launch slowed to let the wave pass and drop us into its trough. Again the engine roared to life, we made a sharp right turn, found smooth water behind a spit of land and were running parallel with the sand beach, which had seemed too close for comfort. About 200 feet behind us the *Filidelphia* crested the same breakers, which were actually a good distance out from the beach.

Both launches cruised along the coast for about three miles before the mouth of the Rio Diquis became visible. We veered upstream into its channel where wild vegetation overhung the river banks. Occasionally we passed grass huts and the children waved enthusiastically as we moved by. The scenery changed and we began motoring by a banana plantation with

Two men cleaned fish and one steered as this locally-built fishing boat was towed behind us upriver to Puerto Cortes.

huge banana trees on both sides of the river and a cable railway spanning the water. A small rowboat was paddled out from the bank and the launch crew tossed a line to tow the boat behind us. While this act of kindness or business was underway the *Filidelphia* tooted past amid cheers of her passengers and groans from ours. Behind us the boatmen cleaned freshly caught fish and washed each carcass in river water.

We left the banana growing area for more jungle and ahead could see the *Filidelphia* swing toward the left bank where in a few minutes we too docked against the mud. Puerto Cortes was an impressive name laid on an isolated plantation village of about 700 people living in a collection of crude buildings and native huts overlooking the river. There was no wharf and a pathway up the high river bank appeared slippery. First off the *Santa Cruz* were those passengers prepared to bargain with a collection of boatmen for passage to the other side of the river where a dilapidated bus was parked. While they negotiated the launch crew tossed their luggage and cargo onto the river bank.

Unloading the BSA involved more worried watchers than there were men balancing the bike onto this narrow gangplank.

It was easy to imagine the gangplank
breaking or the bike falling onto the river bank
as crewmen gently rolled it backward onto solid ground.

My boatman waves goodbye as he returns to Puerto Cortes with a single passenger. Hazards on the narrow footpath included junk and a severe slope.

With this completed thick planks were laid from the *Santa Cruz* to the nearest land. Crewmen spit on their hands and lifted the bike over the water as my heart jumped into my mouth. A quick swing and the back wheel rested on a plank. A moment later the front wheel was on the same plank. But only one man held the machine upright and the muscles of his back strained as the bike began to lean. We all shouted at the same time and other crewmen jumped forward to keep my wheels from toppling into the river. There was a quick shifting of positions so three men steadied the bike as it was slowly edged onto reasonably dry land. My luggage was piled nearby and it became my turn to bargain for a trip across the river.

Some of the boatmen were eliminated from the fun by virtue of sitting in narrow craft that did not seem wide enough to hold the bike. The first price of one that could was ₡25 ($3 U.S.) for all of us to the other side. Hoping that was the highest possible price I asked the owner of the next-largest rowboat. He took the hint and agreed to carry everything to the other bank for only ₡15 ($2 U.S.), which was more in line with what other passengers with cargo had paid. My confidence began to evaporate after I took a close look at the river and my new employee's boat. The Rio Diquis was at least 250 feet wide at Puerto Cortes and its muddy current ran faster than a man could swim. The answer to my query was "50 feet deep." The boat I had hired was about 18 feet long, 30 inches wide and had at least 20 long cracks stuffed with cloth and tar. Water sloshing in the bottom glinted balefully from morning sun and dared me to chance the trip. But there was nothing else to do. I had to get to the railroad on the other side of the river and this was the only transportation.

All the "helpers" who balanced the bike while I walked it up the hill gave the BSA a close inspection and wondered aloud about my destination.

The boatman and his assistant were unable to lift the bike so four "cousins" came to the rescue and the machine was gently lowered into the center of this sure-to-sink transportation. I dropped the prop stand and prayed that it would not punch a hole in the hull. Luggage and cameras were stacked on boards raised above water in the bottom, then the boatmen and I pushed the works out of the muddy shoreline. I was directed to kneel behind the cycle and steady it as the boatmen took position in the front and rear. Their paddles pushed into the mud and we were off. The boat rocked and onlookers, who had stopped all activity to watch, must have held their breath in hopes we would not capsize. But my crew was more capable than I had given them credit for. The rocking stopped and we slid forward smoothly and quietly as they began to paddle. Neither man moved a muscle of his body except his arms, which swung too and fro like mechanical levers. The hull scarcely rolled from their motion as we moved toward the opposite bank. Near the middle of the river the current became stronger and began to push us downstream. From the corner of my eye I watched it churn around us, at the same time visualizing a river bottom about 50 feet below. How could we ever raise my iron if we tipped over? As this unhappy thought mellowed the water slowed, became smooth again and we glided closer to the opposite river bank. When the prow mushed into the mud we all burst into smiles at success of our voyage, which on second thought I imagined the boatmen were not too sure of either.

This side was another narrow shore of mud and grass. A narrow footpath led to the top of the bluff, which was only about ten feet high on this side. Because the three of us could not unload the bike, other boatmen helped lift it out. I carried my luggage to the top and asked them to help me get the BSA up the path. There must have been 20 people balancing that poor little machine up the footpath from hand to hand as I walked beside it and tickled the throttle and clutch to provide forward/upward motion. The men were paid, onlookers thanked for their assistance and everything reloaded while I answered questions about the cycle, my trip and where did I expect to go from there. No wonder they asked. There was only the banana plantation's internal road network and they knew it didn't lead anywhere.

Four miles later I had my first view of a banana-company town. Americanized in appearance and neat to the hilt, Palmara differed from a village in the States in its lack of automobiles and the tropics-style housing built on stilts. I rode around until I found the railroad station and parked on the shady side. Most of it was a freight warehouse with a tiny waiting room near closed ticket windows. A small office in the far corner was for the station master, a Mr. Hunter from Texas.

The first thing he said after acknowledging my introduction was, "How in the hell did you ever get here?" I told him about the trip and asked about transportation to Panama. Hunter told me there really were no roads but a ride could be arranged on his railroad to Golfito. There I could transfer to another line to Puerto Gonzalez on the Panama-Costa Rican border, use a third railroad to Puerto Armuelles in Panama and finally ride the Panamanian government train to David and *La Carretera Interamericana*. It seemed complicated but he assured it was the only route to my destination.

The first step, he said, would be to visit the nearby company office in Palmara, explain my mission and request a pass to ride the next train to Golfito. The office was about a half-mile away so the BSA was kicked to life and off to the boss we went. I had not been able to shave for 24 hours and had slept in my clothes on the launch, which made my first impression something less than imposing. The manager took one look, grunted and allowed as how he was not giving passes to transients. I reported the failure of my mission to Hunter. His boss was condemned to an even-warmer climate and Hunter wrote a pass, which he was only supposed to do for company employees. "But, dammit you deserve one and here it is," he told me.

The train wasn't due to depart for nearly an hour, which gave me time to visit an open-air lunch stand for milk with malt powder, fried corn cakes and a cheese sandwich. My Belgian fellow passengers, who had arrived on the dilapidated bus, were at the counter and we enjoyed conjecturing about what would happen next. I gathered that they were planning to settle on one of the plantations but so far did not know which one. After lunch we moved into the waiting room and baked in tropic heat until the train

Apartments and barracks of the plantations surround a wide playing field on three sides with the railroad bordering the fourth side.

arrived. What a train! A diesel locomotive was coupled to three tired black box cars and four "coaches" constructed from similar black box cars by cutting openings along the sides. The surplus metal had been bent outward to shield passengers from rain and sun. Planks were nailed from side to side in the coaches and passengers climbed over the rows to gain seating.

This didn't seem too sharp and I decided to stay with the bike rather than sweat in such a coach. I rode up a concrete ramp to the second box car where a laborer had laid a piece of sheet iron from ramp to car floor. Inside the bike was parked diagonally on its prop stand. After the train started I was not overjoyed to learn that this car had a flat wheel and weak springs, which caused it to jump up and down as the train meandered along the track. Trying to balance the bike was no snap and the first time we stopped I moved it against a wall so that it could only fall one way. One of the trainmen took pity on me for standing and pulled out his huge pocket knife to cut lashings on a shipment of canvas deck chairs. He extracted one for my use and, sensibly enough, took one for himself. The vibrating car was pleasantly cool while we were moving but the moment we stopped the black paint absorbed every bit of heat in the area. There was nothing to do but sweat it out, which at its worst, was far better than sweating in unison with human sardines in the "coaches."

From the moment we left Palmara the scenery was solid banana trees punctuated every few miles by a small labor-camp settlement where our train usually stopped for passengers or freight exchange. At large camps enterprising individuals serviced train passengers with food and cool drinks. One of the entrepreneurs, a black man, walked by the open box car and I hailed him in English.

"Hey man, how much are the cookies?"

"Boy," he replied, "what you all doing in there?"

"I'm riding back here to watch my motorcycle. What's your name?"

George Bennett had emigrated from Jamaica many years before to work in the Panama Canal area. Then he traveled north for better wages in the banana plantations but because he had no citizenship papers it was difficult to get steady work. His wife baked cookies and he sold them to train passengers to make a living. Unfortunately the train departed before I could buy any cookies.

It was nearly five-hours of nothing but bananas and stops at company towns before we arrived in Golfito. Hunter, who had ridden in the engine, came back to my boxcar and suggested that I park the bike in a nearby warehouse and take my luggage to the guest house.

"Guest house? Where's that?" I asked.

"Head up the street until you pass a clubhouse on the right. The next building is the guest house. Go in, take an empty room, then find the clubhouse manager and tell him you're the man Hunter called about."

The guest house was open and I took one of the two rear rooms. Each had two clean single beds, metal furniture and shared a common bathroom. I showered, shaved and donned clean clothes. The clubhouse manager said that I need only pay ₡32 ($4.25 U.S.) for two days of lodging and could use all of their recreational facilities. Dinner was at six sharp and I was ontime for almost-forgotten state-side cooking.

Afterward I telephoned a Mr. Blair whom I had met in Costa Rica at the Pension Canada. The operator answered in English, knew exactly who I wanted and told me that he was the house guest of E.M. Campbell, executive secretary to the company manager. Blair was pleased to hear from me and insisted I immediately come to the Campbells' house. With his instructions I had little trouble and arrived while they were serving tea and desert...which, of all things, was an excellent banana pie!

The family was intensely interested in my trip and after we talked at length Campbell offered to show me around Golfito. Blair was left with Mrs. Campbell while her husband drove me to the banana pier, which was brilliantly illuminated by huge flood lights. We boarded the nearest freighter, found the bar was locked, watched banana loading for a while and left. He then drove to a lookout point and described the points of interest and distinct sections of Golfito. The length of civilization along the seacoast at the base of beautiful forested mountains was impressive. In one area U.S. citizens lived and played. In another there were offices, warehouses, more homes and recreation centers. A third area was set aside for maintenance yards and freighter loading docks. Here we could see dozens of human ants moving bananas on docks that were margined by blinking lights of harbor buoys. The southern area was where local laborers lived and private enterprises operated, including a small public hotel. As we parted that night Campbell requested that I visit his office the next day.

When the sun blazed into my eyes the following morning I rolled over and covered up for a few minutes more of the first decent rest in three days. After breakfast I paid for my lodging and went to Campbell's air-conditioned office. Up one flight of stairs, turn left and I bumped into Miss Gordon. Perhaps I'd been away from home too long but Miss Gordon was something else. She had arrived in Golfito from Canada less than a year before, did the proper things to a light sweater and smiled as though she meant it. Campbell didn't allow lingering and pulled me into his office to explain that the assistant manager of the facility had approved my visit and the rug was out. A car was at my disposal for the day and Blair would guide me around Golfito to look and photograph as desired.

Downstairs a Ford station wagon and driver were waiting. We picked up Blair and while touring at 10 miles an hour he told me about Golfito the home base for 6500 *bananeros.* Complete within itself, the town supported a huge company store, warehouse, machine shop, golf course, airfield, bottling plant, furniture factory, dairy and bakery, all of which serviced 34 commissaries scattered throughout company property. In the merchandise warehouse, along with the BSA, there was a $500,000 supply of staples. Although variety was limited everything seemed stocked in depth to prevent shortages if incoming ships were delayed. I learned that pricing was on a cost-plus basis so the operation would break even. Foodstuffs appeared to be priced about the same as in state-side markets. Blair explained that savings from buying in quantity were offset by cost of shipping from the U.S. to Costa Rica.

In the maintenance warehouse they had cataloged over 300,000 different items from saddles to coffins, with the emphasis on local purchase or manufacture. It was a fabulous array, with parts for steamshovels binned next to typewriter ribbons. Adjacent repair facilities supported by the warehouse were of equally amazing scope. Behind a simple "Machine Shop" sign was a huge building that seemed to be a complete factory. In one area mechanics were rebuilding engines, truck bodies and batteries. On inside railroad tracks they were repairing huge steam locomotives and passenger

The impressive Golfito installation included railroad yards, maintenance shops and housing scattered in the well-landscaped residential areas.

coaches for the railroad. At the far end of the structure a modern carpenter shop was fabricating a line of distinctive mahogany furniture.

At this time the United Fruit Company had 92,000 employees, over 60 ships and a score of plantations. To demonstrate the policy of working in harmony with the nation of location, the standard of living for Costa Rican workers had been upgraded in a manner consistent with local economic practices. Golfito's wages for local labor were high enough to recruit the best workers but not so high as to dislocate Costa Rica's employment standards. In addition the company had loaned money to private enterprises, which in turn sold their products to the company. Blair's examples were the rice factory, furniture mill, vegetable gardens and leather tannery. Inter-plantation transportation was by railroad while inside Golfito you walked or owned one of the 15 automobiles.

Foundation of all this activity was the banana, usually seen as "hands" of six or eight pieces of fruit at local markets. On a banana plantation the miles and miles of trees averaged 20 feet high and were planted about 15 feet apart. Each growth of the year-round crop, called a "stem," is formed with the bananas pointing upward instead of hanging down as would seem to be the most logical direction. The stem was separated from the tree with one swing of a cutter's machete then four stems were loaded onto a donkey which was led along a pathway of concrete paving blocks to the nearest railroad siding. Each stem was washed before being loaded into cars with slat sides, somewhat like an open top American cattle car. Cutting began early each morning and loading was completed by two or three in the afternoon at which time the cargo (12 tons to a car) was covered with banana leaves. Trains that collected loaded cars from sidings along their route were scheduled onto Golfito's dock by dusk when it was cool and loading could begin.

A short length of narrow timber was all that was needed to ride the bike into a boxcar at the Golfito station.

At the dock, a number of cars were unloaded at one time. Ten stevedores in a "gang" worked only their specific car and as each stem was taken out a company employee made a tally. When a stevedore placed his stem on the endless "gantry conveyer," which carried stems into the ship's hold, he punched a counter to make a separate tally for men of his gang. Because these men earned nearly twice as much as other local labor an accurate stem count was highly important. A ten-man gang could unload nearly 2000 stems an hour and were paid ₡1.50 per man per thousand stems. After stems entered the ship's hold they were stacked with the butt end down and remained that way until the vessel was unloaded at its destination.

Sunday afternoon a Costa Rican came into the guest house and took the other bed. He was about 26 years old and worked as a timekeeper on Farms 47, 48 and 49 for ₡ 450

With the bike in the baggage car,
and the Ford tied down on its flatcar, we're
leaving Golfito on the way to Puerto Armuelles in Panama.

When we reloaded
for the second time the bike was
wired onto the flatcar ahead of the girls' Ford.

At Coto Sur (Southern Landmark) our friendly conductor parked the flatcar on a siding to await the arrival of another engine and car.

($60 U.S.) a month, plus a house and food. He said he was in the fields from six until eleven then completed his reports in the office from one to six. For the three farms there were two timekeepers, one spraymaster, one overseer and 150 laborers. Free motion pictures were shown at the largest farm with the railroad providing transportation to and from evening shows. His arrival in Golfito that afternoon was the beginning of a ten-day vacation that included reserved seating on flights to and from San Jose.

That evening the two French girls from the Pension Canada, Renate and Suzanne, appeared in the dining room for dinner. They told me that a friend of a friend of a friend in San Jose had introduced them to a character who owned a war-surplus landing craft usually used to carry cattle to Golfito. Just by chance he was going to Golfito for a cargo of bananas and would be delighted to transport two such lovely women and their automobile. Neither Renate or Suzanne were exactly babes in the woods and they accepted his offer with a multitude of mental reservations. Somewhere they had picked up young Bob Johnson who was nickle-and-diming through Latin America and invited him to join them at a deserted shoreline south of San Jose where the vessel had been beached. The women claimed that Bob walked to the beach site in less than a day and arrived the moment their car was loaded. (It's more likely that Bob rode with them and was sidetracked in waterfront vegetation until car loading was completed.) Renate laughed while explaining the captain's obvious unhappiness to find that they had a male companion and that his dreams of an overnight trip with two attractive females had gone up in smoke. For 30 hours the little LCP bounded over the Pacific Ocean with one angry captain, two uncaring crew members, three passengers

The engine moved our flatcar
out of the way so it could recouple to
the train and continue on its scheduled run.

At this point the narrow-gauge
rails of the plantation railroad in Panama
meet wide-gauge rails inside Costa Rica.

(L to R) Bob, Renate and Suzanne shared their lunch with me on steps of the telegraph office before we were towed to the Panama/Costa Rica border.

and a Ford sedan. When they arrived at Golfito the afternoon tide was wrong and no dock workers were available to take the car off. The women said they raised so much hell the captain beached his vessel and lowered the ramp just to get rid of them. Bob checked into Golfito's private hotel and the girls found accommodations they had arranged for with United Fruit.

Early monday morning the Costa Rican woke me as I had promised to breakfast with him and wave the flight off. Rising early was well worth while. As the plane departed I enjoyed an outstanding example of animal optimism. The DC-3 started from the far end of a paved runway through the golf course and accelerated about half-way before picking up its wheels. As it rumbled overhead a huge male buzzard roosting on the ridge of a nearby warehouse preened his feathers and strutted along the ridge as if the most beautiful female buzzard in the world was flying past. It was obvious he wondered why she didn't stop for him instead of flying away to San Jose.

Our train was scheduled to leave a few hours later, which gave me good reason to visit Campbell's office for a farewell. He had a pass prepared to carry me to Puerto Armuelles in Panama. The freight warehouse was open when I arrived and it was no problem to ride through into a baggage car, drop the prop stand and mutter a silent prayer everything would remain vertical. The girls' Ford had been loaded on a flatcar, which the switch-engine coupled to my baggage car then added passenger coaches to make up a train. But our scheduled departure had long passed before I learned that the train was delayed because the conductor overslept.

Bob and I were in a coach when Suzanne and Renate wandered in to make it a foursome. Later we joined the Belgians in another coach. Chatting changed to French and I left for the baggage car to see how the bike was doing. Near it the baggage man had stacked several cases of cola on which were cardboard boxes of doughnuts. During a recent lurch the bike had smashed fresh doughnuts into broken pop bottles. The floor of the baggage car was a complete mess, amid which two men were bringing my machinery back onto its wheels as I entered the car. I helped tie the bike to a stanchion then cabbaged a glass-free doughnut and bottle of warm cola.

On my way back to the coaches the conductor stopped to tell me how excited he was to have an author riding on his train and asked if I would mind meeting a few of his friends. I replied that I would be happy to meet anyone who was a friend of his which was probably the wrong thing to say. Within minutes the train went into a snake dance and shuddered to a halt. Though there seemed to be nothing but bananas everywhere the conductor excitedly took my arm and pulled me out of the coach. He directed me to a narrow plank walkway leading toward a somewhat hidden two-storey plantation house about 200 feet from the train. We charged into a roomful of people chattering about why the train had suddenly stopped at their non-station. I was explained and introduced to everyone, most of whom gave me a full and complete account of their work, responsibilities, hopes and plans for life in the hereafter. After ten minutes of this happy confusion the diesel engine gave several sharp blasts and we excused ourselves.

Three miles later the performance was repeated. This time I met the operator of a small company commissary who, the conductor assured me, was not only his very good friend but a "big shot" as well. After this meeting the train traveled 20 minutes before it stopped a third time to meet the engineering superintendent of Golfito. He and his staff had been inspecting the line from the seats of a small gasoline-powered railcar. Of the two of us, I'm certain he was the more surprised. We talked for a few minutes and after I left he must have said something to the conductor because we made no more stops until the train arrived at a transfer point freight platform. This was Coto Sur, the first siding on the railroad between Costa Rica and Panama, where narrow-gauge tracks of the Chiriqui Land Company were paralleled by standard-gauge tracks of Golfito's *Ferrocarril del Sur*.

The bike was rolled onto the freight platform and we were instructed to also unload the Ford from the uncoupled flatcar because very soon a narrow-gauge engine and flatcar would arrive from Panama to pick us up. Our train disappeared through the banana trees leaving the two girls, Bob and me in comparative isolation. We were busy removing wire cables holding the Ford in place when a rumble along the tracks gave notice of an approaching train. Our surprise was compounded to see the recently departed passenger train backing rapidly in our direction. It stopped before smashing into the flatcar and the excitable conductor jumped off the rear coach steps to explain that new orders had been issued. He was to take us closer to Puerto Gonzalez near the border with Panamá.

The windows of every coach bulged with passengers watching us reload the bike and tie the Ford down again. Soon everything was under control and the train towed us through more miles of bananas to the revised stop. This time we were parked on a plantation siding next to a flatcar and locomotive on narrow-gauge tracks. Again we untied the Ford, laid planks between the two cars and Suzanne drove it from one flatcar to the other. The BSA followed. Tiedown of the Ford involved reusing wire from the second, or was it now the third?, exercise. Lunch time was past due and the girls prepared sandwiches, which we ate while sitting on the telegraph office steps. No doubt the trainmen had been watching closely for as the last orange was eaten, which was near-treason on a banana plantation, a man introduced himself as the conductor and said he was now ready to depart. With a magnificent gesture he indicated the extent of his train, which consisted of the enormous diesel locomotive and our very old flatcar on which was one tired Ford and one scruffy motorcycle. We packed our goods, scrambled aboard and rattled off again as a special train of our own.

Now we were on narrow-gauge rails from Panama that extended a short distance into Costa Rica to meet wide-gauge rails of the Golfito plantation line. Our train traveled only a short distance before it stopped by a two-storey building from which hung the national flags of two countries, Costa Rica and Panamá. The building was owned by the United Fruit Company and had been placed so that the international boundary ran through the structure's center. However the architect had not been told of the building's use and his arrangement of bunks had Costa Rican border guards sleeping with their feet inside Panamá.

The Costa Rican immigration control was ready and our passports were soon stamped for passage into Panama. However the *aduanero* had left for a morning siesta and a boy was sent to bring him back. Without his permission neither car nor bike could have crossed the line. Huffing and puffing from overweight and tropic heat the man finally stumbled upstairs to his office where more papers were exhibited, signed, stamped, charged for and returned. Once officially clear of Costa Rica our flatcar was pushed past the border sign to the Panama end of the siding and the diesel engine disappeared back into Costa Rica.

Republica de Costa Rica
Puerto Gonzalez Viquez
Salida...Fecha: 30 Abril 1951

Our flatcar could not be pushed
over the line until everyone's paperwork
was approved by Costa Rican officers in the frontier post.

PANAMA . . . . AT LAST

Republica Panamá...Departmento de Migracion
Tres Pinas...Admitido...30 Abril 1951

The four of us assembled in a tiny office at the Panama end of the building where there were two desks, a white enamel washbowl and a Panamanian officer who inspected papers and signed us into his country. Suzanne tried to find out when our flatcar would be picked up but the man shrugged his shoulders to indicate that he was a government officer and not a plantation worker. She used his telephone to call the Superintendent of the Chiriqui Land Company and request a special train. She was assured that a train would arrive soon in the normal cause of events. Somewhat mollified, Suzanne and Renate led Bob and me to a kiosk for cold drinks at ten cents (U.S.) each.

While at the kiosk I noticed a man standing on the porch of what seemed to be another telegraph office. He was the railroad dispatcher operating out of a two-level office and home who invited us to be his guests until the train arrived. His charming wife was Panamanian by birth and ancestry and he was a Frenchman. Both children were very polite and without obviously being told brought us glasses of ice water. Renate and Suzanne chatted with the wife about fashions while Bob and I visited with her husband. He told us that working hours were from 7 a.m. to 5 p.m. six days a week except when fruit was loaded and his hours were slightly longer. On a responsible job such as this the company provided him with six weeks of paid vacation each year.

The new locomotive is coupled and we're ready to leave Costa Rica and enter Panama. Men sitting near right are in Panama, those standing are in Costa Rica.

Somewhere along the line we picked up cold drinks and carefully parked the empty bottles while Bob took a picture.

His dispatch desk was equipped with an old-fashioned telegraph key and sounder box, telephone and a table radio for entertainment. The telephone headset cord was so long he could stand on the porch to observe and report on distant incoming trains. He was explaining additional details of his work when the telephone rang to announce the impending arrival of our train. At 5:30 a huge diesel-electric locomotive arrived while towing 42 cars of bananas. The train was broken and our flatcar inserted between the engine and banana cars.

After we moved out I climbed into the locomotive and asked the engineer about working on the banana plantation. He told me that with a salary of $125 (U.S.) a month, plus 50% of one month's salary as a bonus in July, and a full month's salary bonus in December, there were few workers who earned as much as he did. Later I worked my way back over the moving train to the first banana car. The brakeman told me he had been with the Chiriqui Land Company for 22 years and was well satisfied. His most interesting comment concerned Panamanian co-workers who, he said, disliked foreigners, didn't work hard enough to justify their wages and thought of nothing but politics. It was pleasant to ride on top of the swaying car where warm air from the locomotive blew over me often enough for comfort. The only disadvantage was the number of large winged bugs that crashed against my back at headlong speed. The two girls had long since fallen asleep in their Ford and Bob was in the locomotive comfortably nodding his head amid warmth of the diesel engine. From a vantage point on top of the car I watched more sights.

Plantation farm communities were spaced along the miles and miles of banana trees. Each was uniformly a "U" of barracks and apartments with a commissary near the railroad and the central grassed area arranged as a sports field. The living quarters were all of the same two-storey wooden construction but despite design similarity there were obvious differences. The most striking variation was that in a few

Wherever our train stopped the BSA would be the subject of intense interest by plantation residents.

communities the buildings seemed poorly maintained and the recreation area weed-grown and unused. More frequently, there were central areas that were neatly trimmed and partially landscaped with manicured baseball and soccer fields. Such neater communities were more often populated by well-dressed people usually wearing brightly colored or all- white clothes.

Occasionally our train reduced speed while entering a large farm. Slowing 43 cars was labor-intensive as the only air brakes were on the locomotive. The hand-brake wheels on each banana car had to be individually tightened by brakemen to reduce speed then loosened as speed was increased. We left the plantation area and its miles of banana trees to pass through typical jungle underbrush before arriving in Puerto Armuelles, headquarters of United Fruit in Panama. Our flatcar was cut from the train, parked on a remote siding and the train left.

No one told us what was to happen next and Renate's Gallic temper flared. She roundly condemned the railroad staff to coal shoveling in hell until Bob suggested she telephone from a nearby line-pole box. Her call was productive. Another locomotive arrived and towed us to an unloading ramp. The cycle was easy and the Ford required little more than caution while driven off the flatcar. I called William Shaffer, manager of Puerto Armuelles, who said that accommodations had been arranged for me as the company's guest. I found the visitor's lodge easily and the manager showed me to a room. Bob wandered in and rented a bed for the night. I showered, relaxed for a few minutes then Bob and I went to the girls' car. In a few minutes Suzanne and Renate appeared from the women's guest quarters and said that someone had told them of a Chinese restaurant. We piled into the Ford for a tour of Puerto Armuelles, most of which was owned by the United Fruit Company. Inside this area there was a four-block-square Panamanian township with saloons, stores, hotels, a Panamanian government office building and the *Ferrocarril Nacional De Chiriqui*. We found the Chinese restaurant for my steak dinner, with pineapple cake ("Pie" on the menu.), for $1.75.

Railroad cars of bananas were pushed to the end of the Puerto Armuelles wharf for nighttime loading into waiting fruit ships.

PANAMA .... AT LAST

Tuesday morning arrived with faint recollections of a midnight quartet drunkenly disharmonizing and disturbing my rest. In addition I was late for breakfast because I neglected to set my watch an hour ahead at the border to match the time-zone change between Costa Rica and Panama. After eating I rode to the township area and arranged passage on the Panamanian government railroad. It had a 1:30 train for David where I could actually get my motorcycle back onto *La Carretera Interamericana*. Ticketing was informal and the railroader more than helpful in making sure I understood exactly what time I was going to depart. Cost of shipping the cycle was $2.85, plus $1.00 for me. I telephoned Shaffer to thank him for his courtesy and explain more about my reasons for traveling in Central America. He suggested that I stay another day or two as guest of the company, a kind offer that was declined with thanks.

During hours remaining I rode around Puerto Armuelles, which was slightly larger than Golfito but less well maintained. Near the ocean there was a complex of workers' housing with dogs and chickens everywhere. It was a constant challenge to avoid hitting one and evading the other. There were few automobiles and the short paved streets had speed bumps every hundred yards or so to enforce the 15 mile-an-hour limit. After running out of things to see I visited the clubhouse for American employees. The library was spotless and seemed relatively untouched by human hands. I read news magazines until lunch, enjoyed a fast meal and searched for the girls and Bob. They were not to be found so I wrote a note explaining my future plans and left it with the waiter who promised faithfully to deliver it to them.

At the railroad station the agent told me to ride around to a loading platform in back where they had spotted my transport. It was a railcar made from a box car by cobbling a driver's cab and engine compartment in front. The rear of the railcar had a doorway so trainmen could move into following cars as though in a passenger train. With advice from idle youths I rode up the loading ramp and squeezed the handlebars through the narrow end door. Inside, the bike was lashed to a wall brace. I had obtained permission to ride with it so the train crew told me to remain aboard while we coupled an ancient box car and departed. The railcar was a genuine monstrosity in which the engine was vented into the driver's cab, which in turn vented through a crawl hole into the cargo section so that all of us were in constant danger of suffocation and fumigation from oil fumes. As speed increased the driveshaft vibrated so violently I stood on tip-toe to keep from being beaten to death. We traveled about six miles then parked to load 65 stems of bananas addressed farther up the line.

65 Of these heavy stems of bananas were loaded into the railcar while the conductor wrote up a waybill in the shade.

This multi-car motor train has switched off the main line on its run to a remote Panamanian village which has no other transportation.

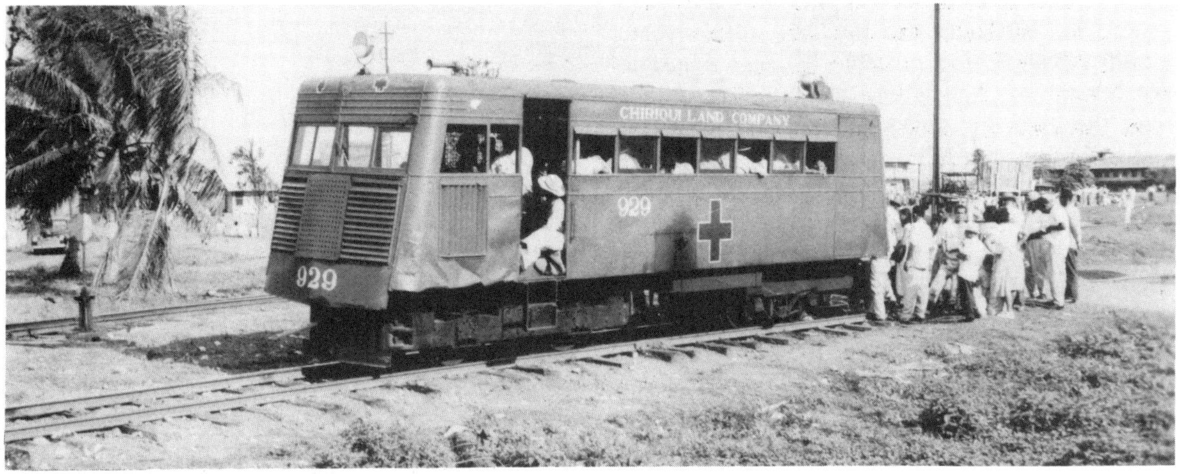

One of several Red Cross cars of the Chiriqui Land Company which provides medical services to its employees living on the scattered banana plantations.

While the train crew worked I took pictures and watched a scheduled passenger railcar pass. After the bananas we moved a few miles to pick up furniture, two dogs and a dozen sacks of corn. In the middle of nowhere the railcar backed into a siding to load a broken water valve being shipped to David shops for repair. As we vibrated back to the main line it began to rain and a pair of hitchhikers boarded for a lift to the next station. There we parked on a siding while a steam locomotive towing passenger cars puffed up the main line in the opposite direction. A mounted policeman came by to eyeball trains and passengers then clattered away along the right-of-way. Train orders were given to our driver and the railcar backed into another siding to couple a flatcar with a Buick wired in place. From here we traveled to La Concepcion and unloaded bananas and sidetracked the Buick.

While this was going on I found a small kiosk at which to buy a glass of milk and piece of cake. Warm rain fell as it became dark and we departed for David. Everything was vibrating well when the truck horn atop the railcar sounded and brakes dragged both feet to stop us in a hurry. Gears clashed as the truck transmission was shoved into reverse and we backed toward the brakeman who had opened a switch so we could park in a weed-covered siding. I poked my head out the open door as a small white motor car chugged past. The railcar driver told me it was one of the two Red Cross hospital cars that cruised the line to bring medical service to isolated villages served only by the railroad. We had sidetracked to give it the right-of-way. More rattling and engine fumes put us back on the main line and at 8:30 that evening we arrived in David. There was no dock or ramp and it took six of us to unload the cycle in a warm drizzle, which was not unpleasant.

I had no idea of where to stay and the station watchman recommended the Pension Chiriqui which was quite a place. My room cost $1 (U.S.) for an area one bed long by six feet wide, inside an eight-foot-high wooden cage covered with chicken wire to keep unwelcomes out. I washed in the grayish basin with water from a cracked pitcher and dined on a ham and cheese sandwich with coffee for 45 cents.

While unloading bananas a tiny passenger railcar of the Panamanian government line rattled past.

In need of a place to park the bike I convinced the bartender that his beer storage room would be ideal. It's possible he agreed just to see how it would get into the building. I rode over the curb and sidewalk, bumped up a few steps, through the lobby and around behind the bar. Racket of the engine inside the old wooden structure caused a half-dozen guests to hurry down stairs to find out what was happening. Then I went to bed, a term which usually describes occupying a piece of furniture suitable for sleeping. Not so here. The Chiriqui's springless wooden box and frame contained only a two-inch-thick straw pad that was almost as soft as the launch bench. In addition, my springless box must have been duplicated in the next room from which a man and woman kept me awake all night. They too seemed to have some trouble sleeping as she continued repeating *"me duele"* ("I hurt."); no doubt from lying on the thin pad.

Early the next morning I worked my way through a half-loaf of good French bread, three scrambled eggs and coffee strong enough to use for engine oil. A nearby gas station filled the tank before I wandered around David (7459 miles) looking for the highway to Panama City. The morning traffic on city streets was heavy with inter-city cargo trucks taking their lane and a half. David had a bustling downtown and early-morning shoppers were everywhere. After I crossed a narrow concrete bridge outside the city limits, an officer of the *Policia Nacional* hailed me to a stop. All he wanted was to inspect the motorcycle ownership certificate and enter my name in a little note book. While this was going on a local user of the highway, riding a donkey, neither stopped, displayed a license plate nor presented ownership papers. Apparently Panama police assume that everyone has a legal right to their own mule.

Because the previous evening drizzle had become an overnight rain the next 50 miles or so were slow going. Though I had ridden in mud before, this muck was deep enough that I paddled more than once to keep upright. Eventually the mud changed to comfortable gravel with enough sharp curves to prevent rapid transit. The countryside appeared lush and usable but there was little cattle-raising, no agricultural activities and few rivers. At Soná I stopped for gasoline at 44¢ a gallon and listened to town kids make snotty remarks about the BSA. From there the routing of *La Carretera Inter-Americana* was delightfully scenic along a range of mountains. I could often view the Pacific Ocean until dark clouds closed in by the time I arrived in Santiago for an overnight.

The main-street hotel gave me a room with an attached shower and permitted lobby parking for the bike. I had finished showering when a tropical storm broke. The street became instant curb-to-curb river as pedestrians scurried for shelter to escape huge raindrops which struck with such force that they bounced five and six feet through an open doorway. The hotel was an interesting building in which all rooms faced an open-air dance floor on one side of which was a cafe and bar. This pleasant arrangement was offset by the floor, walls and ceiling of my room vibrating with thumpings I traced to three large diesel engines in the adjacent municipal electricity plant. Later that evening a young American introduced himself as Bill Pike, owner of the hotel. He explained that during WW II he flew for the U.S. Navy and on discharge came to Panama to seek his fortune. He married the attractive daughter of a Santiago businessman who formerly owned the hotel and other business buildings. Now his wife managed the hotel and Bill operated a flying school, which was unprofitable, and a small airline which was barely paying its way. He also explained that business in Santiago was very bad, their hotel had never been so empty and the Republic of Panama had eight presidents in six years. After Bill left I scanned the local paper, enjoyed a bottle of beer and piled into a comfortable bed for ten hours of vibrating (courtesy of the light plant) sleep.

When the bank opened its door the next morning I was its first customer. A surprise was that my cashed traveler's checks returned United States notes in lieu of the anticipated Panamanian currency. I bought gasoline, promised to write the Pikes (which I did) and left town on a one lane highway of choppy asphalt. This lasted another hour then became smooth concrete in perfect condition. Later I was told the highway had been installed by the U.S. to make sure that military trucks could always reach our wartime airfields along the Panamanian coast. The pavement had been laid with sweeping banked curves that needed only Burma Shave signs to make me feel completely at home. It was followed all the way to the north bank of the Panama Canal where I rode onto a ferry, which carried me across the channel to reach the main highway into Panama City.

It was Thursday, May 4, 1951,
7772 miles and 146 days from Los Angles.

Locks of the Panama Canal,
which are buoyant, open slowly to allow a vessel
to leave the chamber and enter the distant channel.

The Pacific coast remains of Old Panama, founded in 1519, remain as a sad testament to the plundering of the new world by men of all races. It was from here that the treasures of Peru and Mexico were transshipped by muleback across the Isthmus of Panama over a cobblestone path which had been laid through the jungle to Porto Bello, on the Atlantic side. From there the loot was shipped to Spain or England depending on who controlled the port.

In 1671 an English freebooter by the name of Henry Morgan gathered 1400 buccaneers to attack Old Panama. They defeated the Spanish garrison of 2400 men and almost totally destroyed the city in their search for treasure. The present Panama City, located near Ancon hill, was built in 1673 and was never successfully attacked during that period of random warfare and destructive colonization.

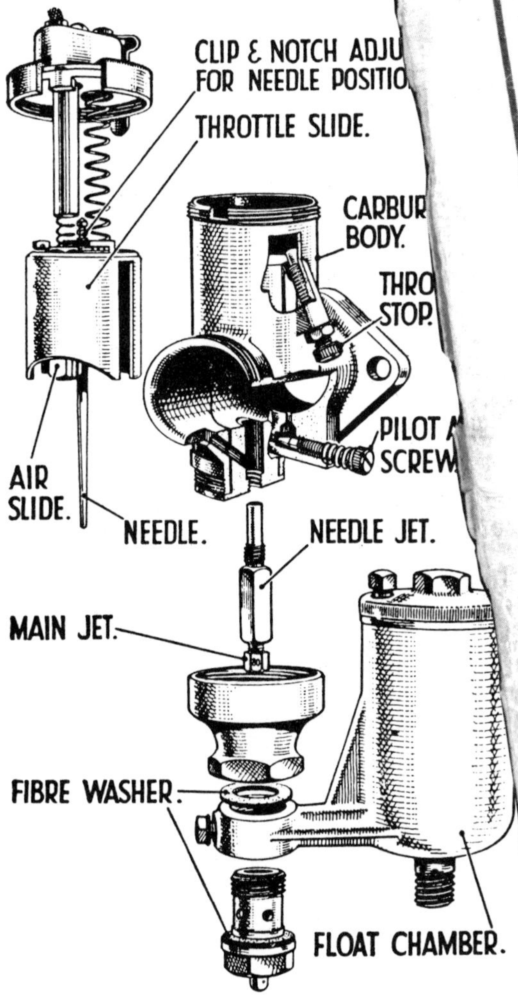

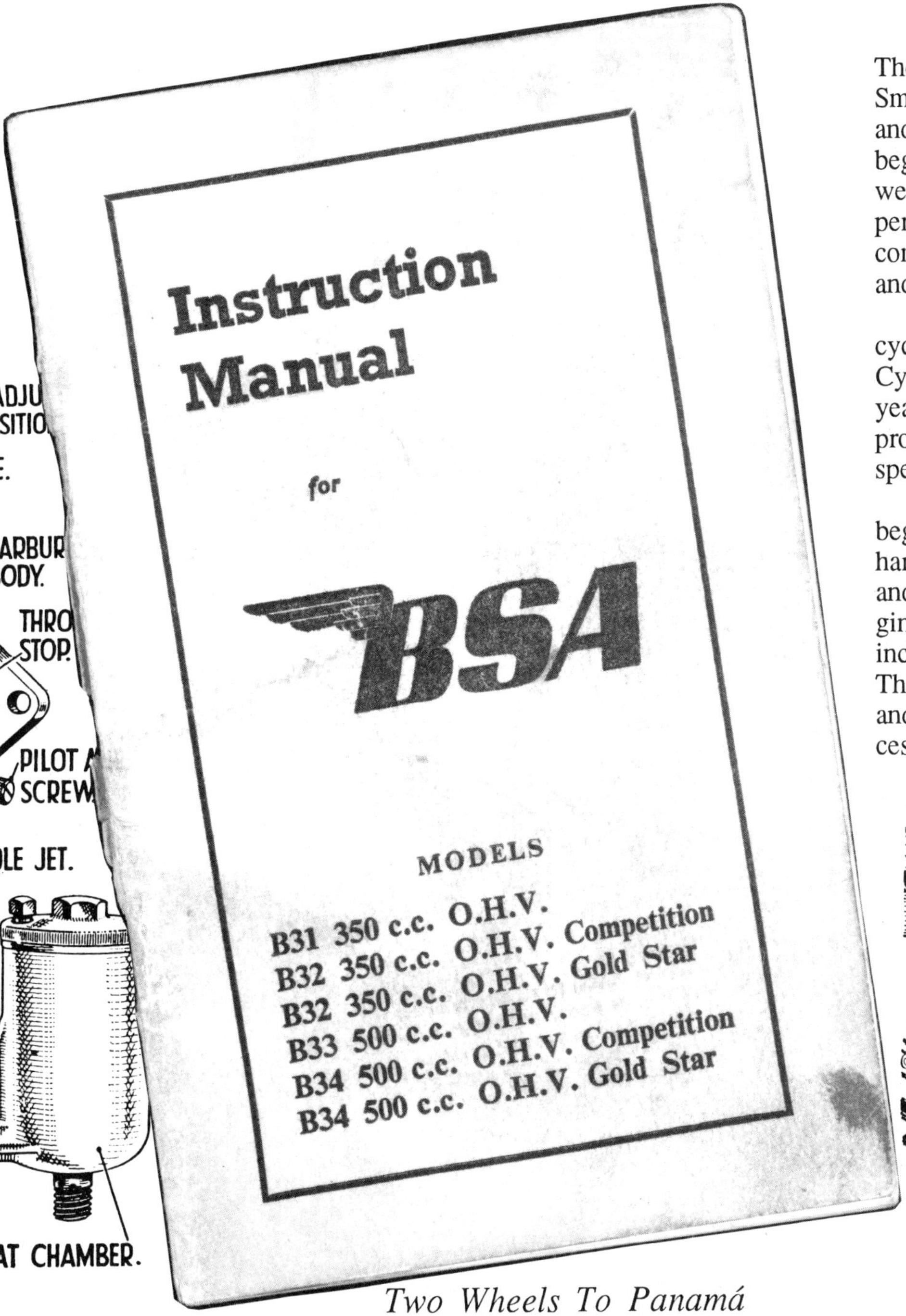

The BSA was an offspring of Birmingham Small Arms the producer of small caliber rifles and sporting weapons. In 1910 the company began the production of motorcycles which were highly regarded for their durability and performance. During the years of WW II the company was a major producer of armament and motorcycles for British military services.

After that period the company's motorcycle production unit was addressed as B.S.A. Cycles, Ltd., of Birmingham, England. In final years the BSA line was matched by motorcycles produced under the Triumph name with specifications close to those of the BSA.

The motorcycle that went to Panama began its production life in 1945 as a 345 cc hardtail single identified as the B31 for touring, and B32 for trials riders. In 1947 factory engineers released a low-cost power upgrade by increasing the cylinder bore to attain 500 cc. This additional series, known as the B33 (road) and B34 (competition) models, were highly successful in trails, endurance and racing events.

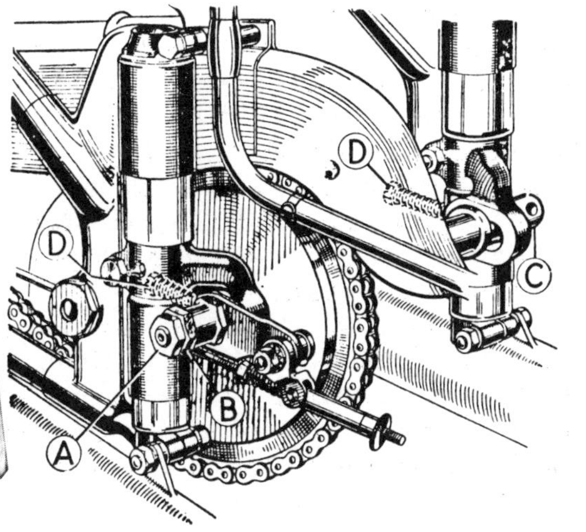

From a historical standpoint it is recognized that from 1945 on there were many B models in the BSA line with variations of rear suspension, cylinder block material, transmission ratios and power output. But the B33 sold as a touring machine was only produced, in its several engine block variations, from 1947 until 1960 when the B-series was discontinued.

During much of this period the standard B33 500 cc single could be ordered with an iron cylinder block, or the aluminum block used for Gold Star engines and with a variety of transmission ratios. For one year only the B33 was offered with the tweaked Gold Star high performance engine and modified carburetion for all out action. Accordingly many an ordinary appearing road machine may be found with an unusual mix of factory performance modifications.

The cast-iron B33 overhead-valve cylinder head was a simple unit that was produced from 1947 to 1960. It was unchanged except for an increase in depth of the fins in 1952 to improve charge cooling in heavy traffic.

An Amal Type 6 carburetor was used on the B33. It was completely troublefree and featured a plunger on the float-valve chamber which could be depressed to flood the carburetor and make starting easier when it was extremely cold. A pancake-type air filter was mounted high on the right side of the frame away from most road dust. It was easily serviced by removing the cap, blowing out the filter element and trusting that it had been cleaned enough to serve for another year of riding.

A gear-driven combination six-volt generator and magneto was mounted on the rear of the B33 cylinder block. The mechanism was troublefree and adjustment of magneto points and timing was easily accomplished by removing the breaker-point cap.

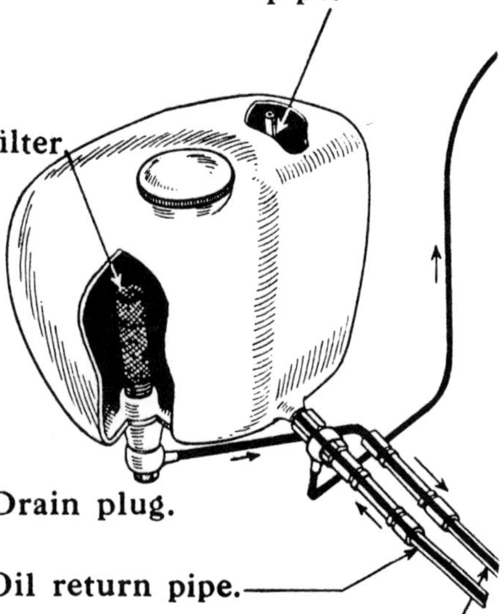

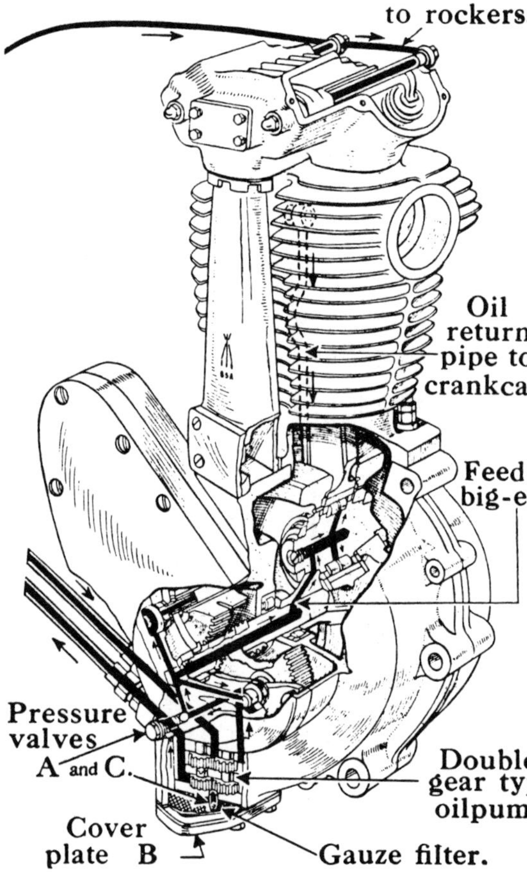

The frame of the B33 was assembled from two separate sections. The lower end of the throat supporting front tube was bolted to a protection bracket attached to the front of the engine case. A frame tube extended from the throat rearward under the fuel tank to meet a vertical tube under the seat which dropped to brackets attached to the transmission case. The rear section of upper and lower tubes contained the rear wheel attachment brackets. This rear assembly was attached to the frame tube below the seat and to the transmission brackets.

In 1949 the factory offered the plunger-type rear suspension as an option on the B models. Both trials (hard) and road (soft) springs were available. Only one spring tension was provided for front forks of production units. Plunger-type rear springing on the B series was discontinued in 1955 when the pivoted swing-frame became standard on trails and road versions of this outstanding series of motorcycles.

THE B33 FROM B.S.A.

The Panama bike's serial number, ZB33-4999, identifies it as a 1950 model and the 999th B33 built that year. It was a well-finished machine with a chrome-plated fuel tank bearing red panels outlined in gold. Knee pads were standard. The front tire was a 3.25 x 19 bias-ply as was the rear in the 3.50 x 19 size.

An excellent book detailing basic maintenance or rebuilding of a BSA single is available as *BSA Singles Restoration* by Roy Bacon. The ISBN Number is 0-85045-709-2.

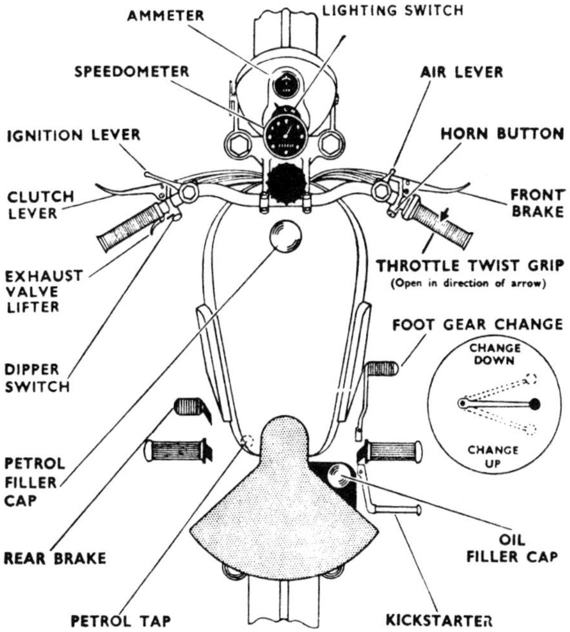

	B31	B32	B32 G.S.	B33	B34	B34 G.S
Petrol tank capacity (gallons)	3	3	*3	3	3	*3
Oil tank capacity (pints)	4	4	*5	4	4	*5
Gearbox capacity (pints)	1	1	1	1	1	1
Bore (mm.)	71	71	71	85	85	85
Stroke (mm.)	88	88	88	88	88	88
Capacity (c.c.)	348	348	348	499	499	499
Tappet clearances (cold) (ins.)	.003	.003	*.003	.003	.003	*.003
Compression ratio	6.5—1	6.5—1	*	6.8—1	6.8—1	*
Piston ring gap (ins.) Max.	.012	.012	.012	.012	.012	.012
Min.	.008	.008	.008	.008	.008	.008
*Valve timing (see page 46) Inlet ..	Opens	25° before t.d.c.		Closes 65° after b.d.c.		
Exhaust ..	Opens	65° before b.d.c.		Closes 25° after t.d.c.		
Ignition timing (fully advanced), piston distance in inches before t.d.c., points open .002ins.	7/16	7/16	*	7/16	7/16	*
Sparking plug	L10S	L10S	*	L10S	L10S	*
Plug points gap (ins.) Max.	.018	.018	.018	.018	.018	.018
Min.	.015	.015	.015	.015	.015	.015
Gear ratios Top	5.6	7.06	*	5.0	5.64	*
Third	7.38	9.30	*	6.59	7.44	*
Second	11.5	14.5	*	10.3	11.59	*
First	16.7	21.1	*	14.9	16.81	*
Front tyre	3.25—19	2.75—21	*2.75—21	3.25—19	2.75—21	*2.75—21
Rear tyre	3.25—19	4.00—19	*4.00—19	3.50—19	4.00—19	*4.00—19
Tyre pressures (p.s.i.) Front	16	22	24	16	23	24
Rear (Solo)	20	16	16	17	16	16
Rear (with pillion passenger)	31	19	19	27	19	19
Chain sizes and number of links—						
Front ($\frac{1}{2}$in. × .305in.)	69	68	—	70	70	—
Rear ($\frac{5}{8}$in. × $\frac{1}{4}$in.)	92	91	—	92	91	—
Engine sprocket (teeth)	17	16	16 to 18	19	20	17 to 21
Gearbox sprocket (teeth)	19	16	16 or 19	19	16	16 or 19
Standard carburetter jet	150	150	*	200	200	*
With air cleaner	150	150	—	170	170	—

Hot roddings early years, when 100 miles an hour over a dusty California dry lake bed was "really moving," come alive again in Bill Carroll's fine book:

Muroc, When the Hot Rods Ran

It pictures everything that happened during the very first of many exciting S.C.T.A. weekend races held north of Los Angeles on Muroc and Rosamond Dry lakes near Mojave, California.

There are over 100 of Carroll's action photographs taken May 15, 1938. They show hot rodding as it really was. Sleeping under the stars, dangerous tuning runs in the dark, early morning speed trials, accidents, contest officials and hundreds of spectators just standing around to watch the rods run. Three official programs list over 500 famous old-time hot rodders. There's a contemporary map, several pages of low-level air views of the races and a copy of the original Southern California Timing Association rules. Everything is skillfully reproduced on art-quality paper in this 80-page, 11 by 8-1/2 inch volume.

Muroc is the perfect companion

for **Two Wheels To Panama** and is a

great motor-history book you'll treasure.

Order your copies today.
$20, plus $2 Packing and shipping.

Personal checks are welcome.
Auto Book Press
P.O.Bin 711, San Marcos, CA 92079

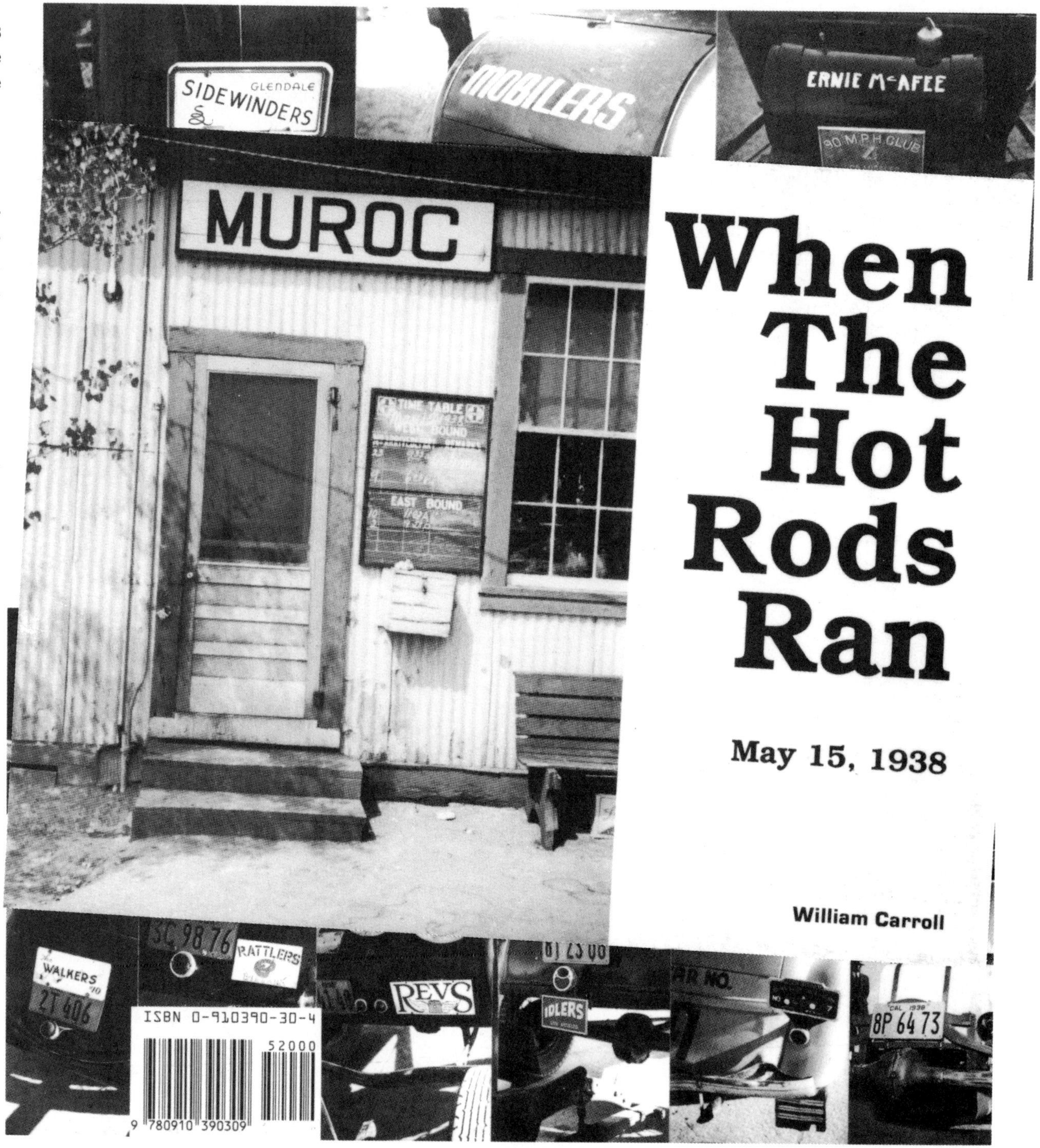